63in63

WITH A LITTLE

DASH

OF CRAZY

THE 63 MARATHONS IN
63 DAYS ADVENTURE

Nikki Love

Dedicated to:

'That Bloke', My SuCKER, Sharif Owadally
I probably could have started it without you but I
probably would have died … but then my story may
have gone viral and now it's your fault that it didn't.
Geez Sharif you suck, thanks a lot!
I love you x

'Boy', My kiddo, Riley Cliff
You are always enough being you.
I love you x

Copyright

Title: With a Little Dash of Crazy: The 63 Marathons in 63 Days Adventure

First published in 2020.

Copyright © 2020 Nikki Love

ISBN: 978-1-8381948-0-2

Cover design: Sharif Owadally

Cover Photo: Nikki Love

For press and PR enquiries please contact the author directly. (http://nikkilove.co.uk/contact/press-pr-enquiries).

Contents

THE ROAD TO THE START

The three most common questions I get asked about my running adventures are:

How do you do them?

Why do you do them? and

Where do you go to the toilet?

I do a lot of primary school talks and, well, kids are curious and have no filters. The last question always comes up, and now that I've brought it up, you're probably wondering where too?

I use the phrases 'I wild wee' and 'I jungle poo' and whilst I'll shed a little more ... discreet ... light on this topic and how I acquired my phrases, you'll be happy to know that I focus a little more on the first two of these questions throughout this story of adventure, challenge and making running dreams real.

So, back to the questions How? and Why?

When I first mentioned to people that I was going to run 63 marathons in 63 days, I was asked these questions a lot.

For me, running 63 marathons in 63 days seemed to be the most logical next step in my life. However, not everyone agreed, and many thought I was perhaps a little crazy.

Here's my potted history of marathon running to this point:

2001 – DNF (Did Not Finish)

2002 – London Marathon

2004 – London Marathon

2010 – 7 marathons in 7 days (the 7th being the London Marathon)

As you can see, attempting 63 marathons in 63 days in 2017 was the most obvious logical step!

Okay, so there may have been a little bit more 'stuff' that went on between 2010 to 2017, mainly the 'stuff' was about me rebuilding my confidence.

Upon completing my 7 marathons in 7 days I was 'encouraged' to put the whole running multi-day thing down and lay it to rest. I'd struggled, it wasn't pretty, it had taken me months to recover. All valid points that perhaps suggested I wasn't good at multi-day running. However, that was other people's thoughts and visions, their boundaries, not specifically mine.

And yet, I did put it down, I was influenced by what other people said and thought about me and my capabilities for a very long time, but sometimes 'time' is a good thing.

In April 2016 I turned 49, which only meant one thing, 50 was next. I wasn't scared of turning 50. I was healthy, fit and looked good for my age (so I was told). It's just that 50 was a pretty big milestone that had kind of crept up on me.

I'd been so busy coaching, training, mentoring, fixing the bodies of other people to help them achieve their goals, dreams and ambitions, that I'd sort of parked up achieving my own.

I came across this saying which really touched a nerve:

'Don't downgrade your dream to match your reality. Upgrade your conviction to match your destiny.'

The realisation of 50 being just around the corner became the catalyst to bringing my running dreams back to life. It was time to find out what I was truly capable of achieving. It was time to go chasing my own extraordinary.

In the leadup to my initial 7in7 I'd read two books in particular that had ignited the thought 'Could I do something like that?'. Those books were *50/50: Secrets I learned running 50 marathons in 50 days – and how you too can achieve super endurance* by Dean Karnazes and *Just a Little Run Around the World* by Rosie Swale

Pope MBE. After my 7in7, I put those books on a shelf and left them there to gather dust.

As my 50th approached, my two favourite adventure books made their way back off the bookshelf and onto my bedside bench and I started dreaming of my own running adventures.

One evening my train of thought went something along the lines of:

'Okay, so I've run seven marathons in seven days, maybe I should run 50, like Dean.'

I then googled the record for most marathons completed by a woman and found an article about a British woman who had recently claimed the Guinness World Record for 'most consecutive marathon distances by a woman' – she'd run 60 in 60 days.

I was thinking big, buoyed from reading my two favourite books and so my thought process continued from there.

'Well 50 is practically 60 and if I'm going to do 60 then I should try to do more.'

I started scribbling.

'If I go on the road for 9 weeks, 9 times 7 is 63. 63 is more than 60. Okay, that's it. That's my target.'

I think I may also have been buoyed by a big glass of red wine that I'd been supping during my internet research and reconnaissance mission. However, I woke up the next morning, turned my notes into a spreadsheet and continued to work on my dream adventure. It hadn't been the red wine; this was a genuine urge to find out what I was truly capable of achieving.

I also had an external purpose. At the end of my 7in7, I had made a promise to my friend Dirk. He'd been diagnosed with Huntington's Disease, and so I promised that if I ever did something as stooopid as 7in7 again, then I would raise money for Huntington's

Disease Association (HDA), the charity helping Dirk live his life with this horrible disease. Running 63 marathons was definitely in the realms of something stooopid, so I figured I could keep my word and make my run an opportunity to raise money and awareness for HDA.

Another question I'm asked is 'Why did I not go for 10 weeks?' to which my reply is '10 weeks? Well that just sounds crazy.'

That didn't mean that I wasn't crazy ambitious about this adventure.

I didn't want to just run 63 days around my house. I wanted it to be an extraordinary adventure. It was my 50th birthday year after all and running for me has always been about the adventure of where my feet can take me.

I chose 63 iconic locations throughout the UK starting at the furthest northern point of the mainland, as obviously it would be all downhill from there. I made sure that the most southern, eastern and westerly points were included, and from there I searched for any established marathon and ultra-marathon race routes at each location that I could use. My plan was gathering momentum.

Next, I needed a crack team to help me.

My 63in63 team consisted of The Asset (that was me), The SuCKER* (my partner Sharif Owadally), The Kiddo (my son Riley Cliff, he stayed home at his dad's doing his GCSE's), and The Coach (Rufus my dog/running partner).

* Sharif soon realised that his working conditions as the person who did everything for me was perhaps above and beyond normal and he wanted to set up a Union for the crew of ultrarunners coining his job title SuCKER ... SUpport Crew Keepers of Endurance Runners. He's still moaning about his working conditions to this very day and trying to build a Union for hard done by crew - good luck with that.

Sharif and I had been deliberating the little issues of 'How was I going to get to the 63 locations?' and 'Where was I going to stay throughout the adventure?'. I didn't have much money; I'd had no luck in contacting hotels for free or even reduced rate accommodation and neither of our cars were suitable to sleep in. We decided my best bet was to scrape together some money and add an extra team member: a van.

Even more ambitiously than choosing 63 iconic marathon locations, and with one week to go, I grabbed my credit card and bought a van off Ebay.

I lived in Nottingham; the van was in Scotland.

'Not a problem', I said as I began organising to collect the van on my way to my start location of John O'Groats, just two days before my start date, unseen and untested by me (or a mechanic) relying purely on the words of the seller that the van was 'good'.

At 9am, give or take half an hour or so as Sharif and I do tend to faff a lot, on Friday 25th August 2017, with everything I thought I'd need for a nine week running adventure squished into Sharif's mighty micra (which is one of the tinsiest little cars on the second hand market) we took off for John O'Groats in the far north of mainland Scotland, via the van owner in Glasgow.

The van was just as the Ebay pictures suggested - old and quirky, just like me.

Only one last thing to do before we got this show on the road and that was to 'Name that Van'. We ran a Facebook competition and as we drove along the east coast of Scotland from Inverness to John O'Groats our newest 63in63 team member was dubbed 'Stan the Van'.

What could go wrong?

Forefront of my mind:
If not now, when? I questioned.
Today, I answer.

~ Nikki Love

WEEK 1

DAY 1. JOHN O'GROATS, CAITHNESS

Sunday 27th August, 2017

Daily distance: 42.2km

Time taken: 5hrs 7mins

Total adventure distance: 42.2km

After travelling for two days and 560 miles through rain, hail, grey and black skies, the wind had finally blown the storm away and the sun beamed on the horizon as we arrived at John O'Groats just in time for the sun to set, and what a sunset it was.

Needing a place to park up our newly acquired home on wheels, Stan the Van, Sharif had been in contact with a local gent, Simon Cottam, who happened to be the owner of the local business, the John O'Groats brewery. We figured that the brewery's car park would be an optimal spot to park the van, being as it was private land and directly opposite the local pub, what more could we ask for?

Something you will get to notice, is that I do like a beer, and as I'd been told that a pale ale was a way of getting a pint of water into me as well as just a teeny touch of alcohol (for medicinal purposes of course), pale ales had become my drink of choice.

It just so happened that the John O'Groats brewery specialised in the making of pale ales, and Simon, who met us shortly after we arrived, kindly gifted us a sample six pack of his brewery's beer. Well, this was a pleasant start to the adventure.

Simon also mentioned he'd be back in the morning to come and run with me 'so long as he didn't chicken out' - his words. He also let it slip that he'd never run further than 10kms in one go in his life, but he was keen to give the marathon a go. I liked his optimism.

As I mentioned, the brewery's car park was opposite the John O'Groats pub so it made perfect sense for us to pop in for some food and to charge all the GPS equipment I was going to be carrying. Oh, and a pint, I may as well start this adventure off on the right foot.

We'd decided that the best tactic to record information to send to Guinness World Records would be for me to carry as many distance and location recording devices that I could. This list included my iphone which I carried in the pocket of my backpack, a Garmin watch that I wore on my left wrist, a Suunto watch attached to the strap of my backpack and a Garmin eTrex GPS which I threw inside my backpack.

We were starting this adventure in the morning with a great big long list of 'things to do' and ideally it would have been great if we'd completed the list prior to starting, but I also knew that there was a big chance that the list would simply get longer if I waited.

Instead I was using the mantra 'If not now, when?' and with that uppermost in my mind I was determined to get going believing that somehow we'd find a way to overcome any obstacles we might come up against. When we collected Stan the Van we'd been told that there seemed to be a problem with the leisure battery, but apart from that the van was good to go, and so sorting Stan's leisure battery nuance was just another task to add to the list that we were going to have to figure out on the road.

Turns out that the leisure battery wasn't the sole issue with Stan, but we'd learn more about that later.

63 marathons in 63 days was now an adventure in action ... onwards 'til the end!

9am start. That was our official 'Start Time' goal and right from the get-go we were running late. As it turned out, it was a pretty rare occasion that I began any of the 63 days on time.

Sharif faffed with the bike that we'd picked up just the day before on our way to John O'Groats. We'd stopped the previous night in Alness, and a wonderful woman we'd met at Alness Parkrun, Aileen Stuart, had asked the question 'Do we need anything?', and quite frankly we'd had 'buy a bike' on the list of things to do, but just hadn't got around to it. She lent us her son's bike and we promised to return it when we were back her way after marathon three.

I faffed with my backpack as Simon, who had turned up and not chickened out, waited patiently for us.

Not only had he turned up, but he'd driven the route we'd planned and dropped water and food parcels along the way. He said he'd see how he'd get on, but this simple action spoke louder and deeper than his words. He was going to go for it! I loved Simon's attitude; it was exactly what I was about to do.

Luckily, his attitude was also pretty good for the practicalities of the run. The route for the day was a great big loop, and with Sharif on a bike being the only logistical support for the day, we didn't really have any other way of getting Simon back to his car other than to run the whole way.

The day started overcast as we took photos at the John O'Groats road sign. Simon had come prepared for the type of weather I was expecting in Scotland, he'd brought a balaclava to protect his head from the elements. However, as the day progressed and the sun regularly peeked out from behind the clouds, his normally practical piece of headgear was proving to be a bit overkill and the sunscreen I'd packed was a little more useful for his Scottish pallor.

My running plan was to run for 5kms at a cruising pace in which I could run and talk without huffing and puffing. At the end of each 5kms I'd stop, eat, water, stretch, and then move on. This plan suited novice marathon runner Simon too.

The first 5kms clicked over and everything was hunky dory. We chatted about why he'd wanted to run a marathon given that, in his words, he wasn't that much of a runner. Turns out that's exactly why he wanted to do it. When he'd mentioned it to his work colleagues and mates they'd scoffed and pointed out that he wasn't much of a runner.

As well as wanting to prove something to himself, he wanted to show his doubters that 'he could'. He also wanted to show his two daughters that taking on challenges was a good thing and that taking action and trying something was better than never giving it a go and always wondering 'what if'.

I had a great big long list of answers to the topic 'WHY did I want to run 63 marathons in 63 days?', and Simon's reasons were aligning very closely to many of mine, which gave us a wonderful conversation foundation to run a very long way.

At the 10km mark, Simon had managed to find the first of his secret 'fuel' stashes. Checking in with how he was feeling, as this was probably the last point in which turning back was going to be the easiest option, he beamed back that he was feeling great and that he was still committed to seeing just how far he could go.

At the halfway mark, Simon was starting to 'feel' the marathon challenge, but he kept on running.

Sharif and I had plotted this route with simplicity first and foremost in mind, no difficult navigation and all on road. We'd take the one road out of town, then it was the second turn right which would take us along the back of the route and then the next turn right would lead us all the way back to the start. For all intents and purposes, it was a simple run around the block, the block just happened to be 42.2kms long. Getting this first marathon under my belt was the target.

Shortly after our second right hand turn of the day and the start of the long road home, I was (the way I remember it) ferociously attacked - a little vole came out of nowhere and tried to kill me.

Now I probably should explain that a vole is perhaps only a tiny bit bigger than a mouse and a little bit smaller than a rat, but in my mind this thing popped out of nowhere and tried to kill me at the ankles. Truthfully it was probably more stunned at running into me, than I was at running into it.

It wobbled about for a little bit, then scurried back into the fields. We joked that the vole would be going home to tell its vole family of its experience of taking on the giant woman.

He'd tell his family that he'd fought a good battle. That he gave her 'what for' and told her to 'stay off his land and away from his loved ones'. He had returned home triumphant and a hero.

Your mind tends to wander and go off into fantasy land when you've been running for a very long time.

At 30kms the borrowed bike Sharif had been riding broke down. The chain snapped. Simon and I stood about for a bit whilst Sharif tried to fix it with our medical kit which consisted of plasters, gauze, sunscreen, Vaseline and ibuprofen.

At the start of the run, we'd told Simon of our policy to 'leave no man behind' which we believed would be a very reassuring policy for Simon. As Sharif was attempting to mend the bike, Simon pointed out that if he didn't keep going, he may not be able to get started again.

Not one day down and we were throwing the 'leave no man behind' policy out the window. Sharif, covered in chain oil, watched as we ran off. I think I may have heard him shout out something to Simon and me as we shuffled off. I'm pretty sure it was a string of complimentary words of encouragement … maybe.

It wasn't long though before we heard Sharif's heavy breathing. He'd given up trying to fix the chain, deciding to just run alongside the bike instead.

He wasn't exactly dressed for running, having donned jeans, a t-shirt and a backpack carrying extra water, food and a med-kit (that did not convert to a bike repair kit). But as he said when he caught up, he'd made a commitment to make sure I made this dream a reality and that he'd find a way to overcome any obstacles. This now involved running in the wrong kit and pushing a broken bike for 12-and-a-bit kilometres. Just so you don't feel too sorry for him, the road was undulating, and he was able to sit on the broken bike and let gravity do the work for part of that distance.

The countryside part of the run had been a bit non-descript but as we hit the coastline, we could see the Orkney Islands, in particular the island of Stroma, from our route. A beautiful thing about running a long distance is that you see the scenery change slowly and how the weather patterns impact the colours of the scenery. I ran along the coastline, mesmerised by the changing colours of the sea and the islands as the sun came in and out of the clouds.

There was less talk and more grunts coming out of Simon by now, but he was finding new depths of his determination that was keeping him going. As we made our way back into town, we were regaled by a highland band which seemed like a very nice touch for John O'Groats to have organised for us. Turns out it wasn't specifically for us, it was the John O'Groats Summer Festival, but hey, it felt like they were playing for us and that the throng of people who had gathered to enjoy the festival were there to cheer us on.

I think the toughest part for Simon was seeing the John O'Groats sign and me saying we had to keep running past it. I was carrying three GPS trackers and I needed all three to reach 26.2 miles. I'd experienced this feeling before of arriving at a designated finish line only to find out I still had a bit more to run.

It hurts!

Simon said he wanted to stop, but there was no way I'd let him come this far and not complete the full distance. He followed me, grunting and groaning as we ran past the sign, continuing out to the end of pier, back to the sign, around the sign several times until my phone and both watches all finally showed 26.2 miles.

I turned and said that's it and Simon dropped to his knees. I don't think I'll ever forget seeing the pure delight, sheer exhaustion and the tears of belief/disbelief, yep both, that he'd completed a full marathon.

As we sat and wiped the tears away, Sharif popped to the van and brought back a few bottles of our gifted John O'Groats Golden Groat beers. Together we cheered Simon, he really had made the impossible, *I'm Possible* and I was so thrilled to have been a part of that moment.

Simon invited us back to his home to take a shower before we left John O'Groats for our next destination. Again, I was privy to a very beautiful experience of Simon proudly telling his wife and daughters that he'd just run a marathon. My heart was so full.

This was a great way to start this adventure, but there was no time to hang about. We, well Sharif, had to drive to our next start line in Tain, which was a two-hour road trip from John O'Groats.

Along the way, we passed through the town of Broro and got a few happy snaps of all the scarecrows around town. I do like me a good ol' scarecrow festival.

We found a layby along a country lane, across from our next day's start line, the Glenmorangie Whisky Distillery. We then found the town chippy for a big serving of fish and chips, which set us up for a good night's sleep. Well I slept, while Sharif tried to work out how to charge all the tech.

DAY 2. TAIN, COUNTY OF ROSS

Monday 28th August, 2017

Daily distance: 43.6km

Time taken: 7hrs 31mins

Total adventure distance: 85.8km

Waking up in the van and opening the doors to the countryside of the Scottish Highlands is a bit special. Quiet, peaceful, beautiful.

Waking up in a van that we'd literally thrown all of our stuff into two days previous and was still trying to sort – well that was not so special, but it was an 'adventure'.

The bed was a little too short for Sharif, which didn't bother us both too much (and when I say us, I mean me). What bothered 'us' was the width of the bed – I'm a tosser, a turner, a starfish sleeper. This was going to be a potential problem.

We were also trying to work out where to store all the things that I'd thought necessary to bring, which in hindsight was way too much. On a positive note, Sharif had managed to get the stove to work to make bacon and eggs for breakfast, and the kettle to boil water to make filtered coffee and commence the morning ritual of waking me up and making me a coherent (and friendly) human being.

The night before we had pondered whether we had parked up on a lane way or the driveway to someone's house, but too tired to worry too much we set up camp and hoped we wouldn't be asked to 'get off my land'. A car meandered its way down the laneway as I was having my morning coffee and enjoying the view, they simply gave us a wave and carried on.

It was going to take a little bit of time getting used to the van. Sleeping. Eating. Moving about. Luckily, I had 62 more days to get used to it. With breakfast eaten and food prepped for the day, Sharif drove the van the few hundred meters from our camp spot to the Glenmorangie Whisky Distillery visitor's car park that was going to be my day two start line.

We popped in to check with management that it was still okay for us to leave the van in the car park without actually visiting the centre or taking the tour. Another day maybe, but not today, to-day was all about marathon two.

9:00am start – yeah right. We set off about fifteen mins later than planned due to our morning faffing.

Today's route was going to be a two-loop circuit up and around Tain Hill. The plan was that Sharif would run the first loop with me so that I could get used to using the eTrex GPS that we had bought to plot routes, but not tested. Testing was one of those tasks on the 'to do list'. It wasn't that we thought the tech needed to be tested, the tech was fine. It was all about me being a tech-luddite and potentially not being able to navigate myself in the right direction. The intentions for the second loop was for me to run on my own so that Sharif could sort the van.

It was a beautiful location for a run, if a bit hilly, perhaps the name Tain Hill should have given us some sort of heads up that this was not going to be an easy run. Easy no, but scenic, absolutely, with the route taking us through acres upon acres of Forestry lands which had acres upon acres of enormous pine trees all lined up in a row.

The bonus of a hill is that it usually brings some pretty vistas and the vistas of the coastline, the surrounding mountains, the clouds sweeping across the sky, the sun-showers that brought rainbow after rainbow, was truly worth the effort of the upwards climbs.

Whilst we'd had a spot or two of rain during our morning, we were being spoilt with a patch of some unseasonably warm weather. However, the week before the weather had been more typically 'Scottish' and many of the trail paths we'd planned to run along were quite wet and boggy. A few turn backs and alternative paths chosen meant that the first loop didn't look quite like the route map that Sharif had plotted for me to run. As such, as well as relying on the GPS tech I was carrying, we thought it would be a good idea to go a little old school and put stones and twigs in arrow formations at trail intersections so that I would hopefully choose the right direction when I was on my own on the second loop.

As we came to the point when Sharif was going to wave me off to go finish the second loop on my own, he suggested that maybe he should perhaps tag along with me, just to make sure I didn't get lost. I was glad of the company, it was a beautiful run, but it had been quite quiet and isolated.

Although we knew that Sharif was going to run a whole marathon with me at some stage of the 63 days, we'd anticipated it would be a few weeks into this adventure. Instead, by staying with me on the second loop, marathon two for me was going to be his first marathon. Two newbie marathoners in two days, I was thrilled.

On the second summit of Tain Hill, we stopped to take some happy snaps in a picnic area that really was the perfect location for capturing the stunning vista. Noticing another couple actually picnicking, Sharif said, and it was a comment that he was going to repeat over and over and over again, 'Can we come back here and enjoy where we are and what we're seeing without the running please, perhaps, like normal people'.

I looked over at the couple, and I agreed that it was a lovely thought, but then I pointed out that this was going to be the norm for us and perhaps he'd better get used to it. He smiled and we ran on.

With the marathon distance nearly complete, we realised that we had to up the pace a little. I wasn't particularly interested in running any specific times during this adventure, getting through each day was the aim, but the Glenmorangie Whisky Distillery car park had a specific closing time and we had to get the van out of there or we'd be doing marathon three in the same location.

I'm not sure how we both found that extra gear, me on my second marathon and Sharif on his first marathon, but we did and got to the car park minutes before closing time which was fine for sorting the van, but we both hadn't reached our target distance and I really wanted the finish line photo to be in front of the distinctive signage of the distillery. I continued running around the car park as Sharif paused his watch, grabbed the van and drove back to our previous evening's layby. He restarted his watch, ran back and joined my circling pattern.

We may have looked a little bit odd running around an empty car park, but it was worth it when we finally achieved the full marathon distance and got our finish line happy snap. It was only then that we realised that we'd have to run back to the van that was now parked a bit of a ways down the road. This was going to be a recurring theme, I'd either have to run around in circles a few times at my finish location to make sure I covered the full distance or I'd have to run beyond the marathon distance because I hadn't quite made it back to the van.

Food time. We'd made the decision that we'd buy our dinner food at the end of the day from the local supermarket, the local chippy or the local pub. Today it was the local supermarket.

We shuffled along the supermarket aisles with silly grins on our faces, we were both pretty proud of ourselves. I'd run my second marathon in a row and was feeling pretty good and Sharif had run his first marathon and was feeling on top of the world.

He was there helping me make my goal dream come true, but he was also going to make one of his own dream goals a reality. He'd made a promise to himself to run five marathons before he turned 45. He was 43 and he'd officially kicked off his campaign in a stunning location.

With food bought, we started our daily Facebook live completion video. Looking into my camera I gave a little gasp, oh man I was sunburnt, this really was not what I had expected from the Scottish Highlands. Applying sunscreen was going to be added to the daily routine checklist that we were starting to put together for this adventure.

As we hovered around the van, a bloke pulled up alongside us and asked what we were doing, he'd noticed the big Huntington's Disease Association (HDA) sign on the back of our van. We told him our story and he told us his. His family was affected by HDA, his sister was in the grips of the disease. It was only a brief conversation, but it was enough to see his immense sorrow for his sister and the pain that this disease causes.

I watched him as he talked, he had a few little arm twitches, body movements, speech ticks, which I knew were early symptoms of Huntington's, but I had hoped were not in this case. We wished him and his family well, he said he'd follow along as this was so important to him.

About a year after I'd finished this run, the bloke from the Tain car park got in touch with me to say that he had been diagnosed and that he too had HD. He thanked me for the work I'd done in raising money and awareness. Huntington's really is a horrible disease in which the person slowly but surely loses control of the use of their body, their speech and their mind, his news brought me to tears.

What are the right words to say – are there any? I said I was sorry to hear his news and that I was sending him my love and thoughts.

DAY 3.   LOCH NESS, INVERNESS

Tuesday 29th August, 2017

Daily distance: 42.8km

Time taken: 5hrs 29mins

Total adventure distance: 128.6km

My parents are Scottish, very proud Scottish although they now reside in Australia, and I was mainly brought up with the comments and imagery that Glasgow (where they were born and raised), and in turn Scotland, was always cold, grey and bleak pretty much all the year round. Although we were yet to get to Glasgow, I was learning quickly that the imagery I'd been raised on was far from the reality I was experiencing.

As well as the grey and dank stories of the streets of Glasgow, I'd also been raised on stories of Loch Ness and its mythical monster Nessie. The images I had were of a body of water that was always dark, eerie and scary, the perfect place for a monster to live. I guess I was about to experience the reality of these images too.

Today's route was the actual course of the Loch Ness marathon. A point-to-point race starting in what appeared to be, as we drove up and down the road looking for a significant sign or landmark that could have warranted a start location, in the middle of nowhere.

Whilst the start was not that auspicious, as I followed the route along the bank of Loch Ness, I can quite categorically state that the rest of the day was.

Sharif was going to drive the van today. The intention was that he'd drive on ahead for 10kms, park up, prepare me some food and wait until I reached him. He'd then hand me some food and drink and repeat this process the whole way to Inverness.

This plan soon went out the window when we saw just how stunning, but sometimes a little dangerous, the road along Loch Ness was. The road was a little windy and, in some places, had no verge for me to run along. During the actual marathon, this road would be closed for runners but as this was just me doing my own sweet thang I had to deal with the traffic.

Worried that drivers may be paying more attention to the scenery than to someone running along the edge of a road, Sharif alternated his driving tactics. Where the road was good and there was a verge, he left me to it, driving on ahead and waiting up. When there was no verge, he drove behind me with a hastily scrawled sign on the back of the van stating 'runner ahead'.

Thankfully it was mid-week, so the traffic was minimal and those that were driving didn't seem to be in that much of a rush. We did get a few toots, but I think they were toots of support. Most people were happy to slow it down and only pass me when it was safe for us both.

I'd really wanted this adventure to be a running tour of this beautiful land, and I really was touristing my little heart out. I was snap happy. I kept stopping to get a photo of this brook, that river, this angle of the Loch, that angle of the mountains. I was truly in awe of just how beautiful this part of the world is, the sights were breath-taking, almost to the point of distraction. I ran past a sign for a waterfall. Oh wow, I definitely have to see that. I'll just divert over here and climb down all these steps so that I can get a better look … is how my day went.

As I ran, the sky changed from cloudy, drizzly and misty, to clear with stunning blue skies, then back to a mix of clear sky with clouds that held every shade from white to grey. As the sun came out, the Loch glistened, sparkled and twinkled as the sun caught the chop of the water, and the surrounding hills, covered in thick dense trees, lit up. As the clouds rolled over, the waters darkened, the surrounding hills took on a menacing look and I kept imagining that this was the time I'd see the emergence of a tail, a head, or a hump of the infamous monster. Alas, I had no sightings of Nessie, but all through the day Mother Nature provided me with the most stunning scenery, each change of weather creating the most beautiful piece of art that I seared into my memory or captured on my camera.

As well as feed me, water me, point me in the right direction, drive behind me for safety, drive ahead of me for motivation and navigation, Sharif also had to remind me to stop taking so many photos and selfies and get on with the running bit. Yes, I could enjoy myself and I could appreciate my surrounds, but I had a distance deadline to achieve every day.

Once past the Loch the road to Inverness was pretty much a road which allowed me to get down to business. Sharif headed off to park up Stan whilst I made my way back into civilisation and towards today's finish line.

Thankfully Sharif made a 'chief in charge of logistics' decision. The official marathon's finish line was at Inverness Castle and the thing with castles is that they are generally built on hills and Inverness castle was no exception.

Rather than do that to me, oh he was good, Sharif parked up along the River Ness, walked towards me as I shuffled along and suggested a diversion over the bridge to the opposite side of the river rather than up the hill, thus keeping the surroundings beautiful and the elevation low.

As I finished my last couple of kilometres, I watched some keen folk in their waterproofs standing in the river fly fishing.

What a good idea. Think I'll have me some of that as soon as I finish – the water, not the fly fishing. Cold water therapy is a recommended recovery method for aching muscles and it's one I have used in the past. The sun was now shining brightly, the River Ness was looking inviting and with my 42.2kms done, I took off my trainers and socks and wandered into the edge of the river.

Holy guacamole it was cold. This was just as cold as any ice bath I'd ever experienced, and I was quickly remembering how much I really did not enjoy cold water therapy.

I gave out a little squeal with every step I took into the river. I managed to go to the depth of mid-shins. I knew the process was to calm down and breath and get used to the water, but that was going to have to do me. It was absolutely brrrrfreezing.

A drizzly start, a spectacular landscape through the middle, a beautiful city to finish in and a little ice therapy session in sunshine to end. What a day!

An old work colleague of Sharif, Marcin Polata and his wife Gabi, had kindly put us up the night before offering us their home, their kitchen and booting their son, Nick, out of his bedroom, to accommodate us. Marcin and Gabi kindly offered a second night which meant a very short trip from today's finish line to a comfy bed, a lovely home-cooked meal and a good night's sleep.

We did love Stan, but we were having a few teething problems with him. I guess that's what you get when you pick up a van, untested and unseen, a couple of days before you start an epic adventure. And what's an adventure without a few potential problems and dubious decisions?

DAY 4.   AVIEMORE, INVERNESS

Wednesday 30th August, 2017

Daily distance: 42.4km

Time taken: 5hrs 35mins

Total adventure distance: 171km

Marathon number four had been one of my mental 'hump' days that I was keen to get through and prove to myself that I was capable of doing this challenge.

Up to this point in my running life, I had completed two multi-day events and on both occasions my day three had ended with my body feeling pretty beaten up and my day four on both occasions had been completed in agony.

The first multi-day event was my seven marathons in seven days which I did way back in 2010. By the end of day three, I was in agony both physically and mentally. I had only ever completed two marathons prior to that challenge, and I'd taken a two-year recovery gap in between both of them.

Despite my lack of marathon experience I had come up with the idea that I would be able to run 7in7. However, by the end of day three, my body was shouting at me that perhaps this had been a bad idea. I'd never experienced knee pain whilst running and holy moly, my knees were in agony and my whole body was aching.

I discovered depths of determination, persistence and resilience that I never knew I had. Despite being in agony from day four onwards, I did make it to the end of marathon seven and on day eight, I literally lay in bed and couldn't move. It took me months before I felt strong enough to run again, but oh man was I proud that I never gave up.

Luckily, time heals, memories fade and somehow, when I had gathered enough courage to take on another multi-day adventure, I'd managed to forget all about that pain. I should point out that it was six years later, and perhaps enough wine and beer had been consumed in the interim to dull the memory.

The next multi-day event I entered was in Peru, and boy was it was a doozy.

In 2016 I booked myself into a race called the JungleUltra. It was a 250km, 5-day race in which you are required carry everything you needed to survive, in your backpack. This included a hammock tent, sleeping bag, food for five days, campsite clothes, essential survival and medical kit and a minimum of 2 litres of water (which was provided daily and replenished at each checkpoint).

As I mentioned, all of this was kept in a backpack that you carried as you ran through the Amazon jungle of Peru.

In this instance, on day three I was feeling awesome and I was 5kms into my day when I heard a POP! I'd gone over on my ankle. Owwww, that smarted.

I stopped for a little rest to let the first flood of pain ease and put my weight back on my left ankle. It hurt, but it felt bearable … just. I'd come a long way to give up at this early stage of the adventure. I figured I hadn't broken it, as I could still put weight on it, but golly it hurt some. But that's when adrenaline kicks in. I figured, if I kept going to the next checkpoint the medics would be there to have a look and provide me with a dose of pain killers.

Each and every time I landed unevenly on my left ankle, and there were lots of times, the pain seared. The thing about running through a jungle is that the path is not clear, it's not even, and it is definitely not easy, but I managed to keep going for the remaining 35kms and made it to the end of day's campsite.

The medics suggested I keep my shoes on until they were ready to do the nightly repair and maintenance of all the runner's feet and bodies. A little aside, I had blisters and rashes and cuts and bruises all over my body, and in many nooks and crannies that I hadn't expected, that I'd coped with up to this point.

I hobbled over to the campsite, dropped my backpack, hung up my hammock tent, then hobbled to the cold shower area to attempt to wash off all the mud I'd collected from the jungle whilst I kept my shoe on. I prepped my dehydrated meal and finally got out of my running kit and into my camp clothes which consisted of leggings, a singlet top and thongs. Now, when I say thongs, I do mean the things us Aussies wear on our feet, if you're British I'm referring to flip flops not underwear, there was no room for camp underwear in my backpack, remember we had to carry everything we had brought with us for the entire 250kms.

By the time I took my foot out of my trainer, my ankle was quite a size.

That evening I got the verdict from the head of the medic team, Exile Medics. Torn ligaments 'yes' but broken bone, most likely 'no'. This was all I needed to know. I was adamant that I would continue and manage the pain with medication and my self-belief that I would get through this, and I hobbled off to my hammock.

My day four during my 7in7 and the JungleUltra was probably the worst I had ever felt whilst running, but I survived them.

Right here and right now in Scotland, my day four was panning out to be a different story. No injuries, woohoo! No aches or pains other than a little stiffness and tiredness which I could handle, and I had another stunningly beautiful location to get stuck into.

Today's run was at Aviemore, in the Cairngorms.

All I knew of Aviemore was that it was a place in Scotland to go skiing when the snow falls enough to cover the mountains but not too much that it stops the traffic from getting to the mountains. I'd heard this was quite a common occurrence. Snow was currently not an issue as the Highlands of Scotland was having a belter of an Indian summer and today was going to be another gorgeous day.

As we drove into Aviemore we noticed the number of cycle shops, as it turns out Aviemore is also renowned for its off-road cycle paths which is what I would be running along for most of the day.

The previous evening we'd returned the bike that we'd borrowed on our way to John O'Groats, apologising profusely for returning it in a less useable condition than which we'd collected it.

Buying a bike had been on our list of 'things to do' before we started. We thought it would be a good tactic having Sharif ride alongside me to carry food and water, and it had been for the first 30 kilometres of marathon one until our borrowed bike broke. As Aviemore appeared to have an abundance of cycle shops, the task of buying a bike was bumped up the list from a 'to do', to a 'today'.

Just prior to starting this adventure, we'd set up a funding page via PledgeSport. The money raised on this platform was to help me fund the trip in return for some rewards. In total, over the nine weeks, we raised £1,650 which helped go towards the costs of petrol, food, my trainers and this soon to be purchased support bike.

It was a drop in the ocean in terms of the total cost of the adventure – along the way my credit cards were maxed out and Sharif's parents were often tapped up for loans to pay for petrol and food as we struggled to hold on until his next payday, but the cost was an accepted risk on my behalf and the financial help we did receive was genuinely appreciated.

Starting at Loch Morlich, the plan was for me to run a loop to the town centre of Aviemore and back and I'd then finish whatever distance remained looping around the Loch. Meanwhile, Sharif would be a man on a mission to buy a bike. By the time I reached our rendezvous point in town, we had a new 63in63 team member – Scotty the Bike.

I was in a running flow, feeling good and loving the gorgeous forest surrounds. I do love trees. To look at, to run through, to climb up, to breath in.

There's a Japanese phrase 'Shinrin-Yoku' meaning forest bathing. Spending mindful time in woods, in forest, in green spaces. It's often prescribed by Japanese doctors to counter illnesses such as depression, anxiety, stress. I know that I feel lighter in worries, stronger in mind, and more purposeful every time I enter some wood, a forest or even a clump of trees. Running the cycle paths around Aviemore definitely put me in a happy, strong and confident mood.

Standing looking up at the height of trees around me, I could feel their age, their strength and their history, I could feel it being absorbed into me and I took a moment to reflect.

I was going to get through this adventure. I knew my purposes were strong - to raise money for charity, to see this wonderful country, and to connect with my internal strength and power.

I knew I had a long way to go, but I also knew that I was going to give it everything I had to get through. Everything!

I made it back to Loch Morlich to coincide with my half-way point of the day, and Sharif was waiting with some food and his running kit. Given that he'd had a rest day yesterday, he fancied a little run about and the path around the Loch looked stunning.

Not long after I first met Sharif, he had offered his help with the planning for this adventure, if I needed it, as a friend.

I know that driving me to the other end of the country, being my support crew, feeding, watering, putting me to bed, waking me up, pointing me in the right direction and then running in the most stunning locations of the UK was probably not what he had originally had in mind with his almost flippant offer of help, but things escalated quickly between us in the four months after we met. We were now four days into this enormous adventure and having Sharif's company during my runs, I couldn't imagine experiencing it with anyone else in any other way.

As we ran around the Loch I was wondering if my eyes were deceiving me ... a sandy beach with people sunbathing. The pier end of the Loch looked a lot like a beach. Oooh it was.

At 300m above sea-level, the signs at the water's edge proudly boasted that it was the highest beach in Britain.

As much as I wanted to have a little laydown and a sunbathe, after all one of my biggest goals in life is to be a lazy-assed beach bum, for now I had to keep on trucking as I'd received a lovely offer of a complimentary massage from Kirsty Wright whose sports therapy clinic was based at Glenmore Lodge. All I had to do was get to the centre before closing time and although I was running steady, I was slow, and finishing by closing time was going to be a push. Definitely no time for sunbathing.

The offer of a massage was too good to miss, so as we passed the van, Sharif got on Scotty the Bike and cycled next to me urging me to push a little harder and go a little bit faster on the final loop of the Loch.

It was worth it. Katie was a wonderful therapist who'd had plenty of experience working on the legs of many an endurance athlete. She understood that I had to get back up again and run the next day, so the massage was a balancing act between deep, but not too aggressive, care. My legs were absolutely loving the servicing they were being given by Katie and to finish off a stunning day, Sharif treated me to the bestest and biggest burger in town.

I'd faced my day four nemesis and was feeling pretty darn good about it.

We had a long drive ahead. Well Sharif did. I was ready for that laydown, and as much as the beach appealed, the back of the van was going to have to do. I was coping but I needed sleep.

We pulled into the Premier Inn Hotel car park at Fort William which was going to be our home for the night. We didn't have a room, but we were given permission to charge all of our tech in the hotel lobby and stay outside in Stan the Van.

So far so good.

DAY 5.   FORT WILLIAM, INVERNESS

Thursday 31st August, 2017

Daily distance: 42.6km

Time taken: 5hrs 46mins

Total adventure distance: 213.6km

Life on the road in a van that we'd picked up just two days before my first marathon and that we had quite literally thrown all of our stuff into, was tough getting used to.

The van was a mess, we both looked quite a sight of dishevelment, but this was all part of the adventure. I was testing my endurance. Sharif was testing his project management skills. The van was testing its ability to cope with the distance and housing two rough, smelly and tired inhabitants.

We knew we needed routine, and we'd created a simple one:

Wake me up. Wake me up again after I'd fallen back asleep. Coffee, breakfast, dress, stretch, pack back-pack, run, eat, run, eat, run, stop, eat, drive, eat, sleep.

It was tough, for whilst I was able to get up and run each day, I was struggling to do much more at the end of the day other than eat and collapse.

The original plan for week two of this adventure was that I was going to be on my own. Sharif would head back home to Nottingham to go back to work and I'd keep up my daily marathon, then drive to the next location which was anything between two and three hours of driving, and feed myself and rest and recover for the next day.

As we were getting closer to our originally scheduled goodbye day, we were realising that the initial plan for me to carry on alone was perhaps not a good one. I'm often asked, 'What do you think about when you run?' This was going to be today's topic of thought and discussion with Sharif, 'How was I going to keep going?' The only thing I knew for certain was that I was going to find a way.

We woke up in the car park of the Fort William Premier Inn and, as far as car parks go, it was functional, but as far as views of surrounds go, it was spectacular. What a view to wake up to: Ben Nevis was in the nearby distance and although the morning fog was clouding the tops of the ranges, what we could see provided enough of a teaser to know that the views today were going to be awesome. This was going to be some sightseeing marathon.

Thankfully, the route I'd planned was not going directly up the mountain. Ben Nevis is the highest mountain in the UK with a summit rising to 1,345 metres above sea level. I was ambitious, but not that ambitious. Instead I was going to run along some low-level mountain bike tracks that headed down towards the River Lochy and the Caledonian Canal.

Sharif was very excited, the network of trails around Nevis Range, known as 'The Witch's Trails', were world-class quality and he was going to really get to test out our newest team member, Scotty the Bike.

I was excited because I was going to be running quite a distance along a canal. The beauty of a canal is that the land alongside it tends to be relatively flat(ish), and any changes in elevation tends to be a short rise on the path alongside a canal lock. Today was the start of what was going to become quite a love affair for me with canals.

In terms of running pace, I had decided that I was going to run at a cruising pace of 6kms per hour which factored in short walking breaks in which I could eat and drink on the move. This generally meant that I'd be on my feet running for around seven hours per day.

When I tell people that time often flies by when I'm running, they wonder how.

One of the best tips I was given as I was getting ready to run through the Peruvian jungle was from a lovely chap, Dale Thomas. Running through the Amazon was quite frankly scaring the crap out of me and I was feeling more than a little overwhelmed. Dale had been there the year before, he knew what we were about to face and he calmly said to me, 'When it all feels too much, don't forget to look up'.

It's a message that I now pass on to others and reinforce myself with regularly.

Look up and take it all in, give thanks for the opportunity you have created, appreciate the beauty of where your feet can take you, smile, breath and then get moving again.

My backpack was filled with my food, water, cameras, phone, GPS trackers and wet weather clothes, and I was ready to roll. As I scootched along the mountain bike paths I was constantly looking up and seeing the wilderness around me. Yes, it was woods and yesterday I had run in woods, but no two woods are ever the same, and no two days in the same woods are ever the same. The weather, the light, the movement of the trees, the movement of the woodland wildlife all change the view, the perspective, and the feeling of each step of each run.

Running in nature is what my version of heaven looks like.

As I emerged out of the Nevis Range and headed along the road towards the River Lochy I noticed that the morning fog had lifted and I was able to get a full look at Ben Nevis and the surrounding ranges.

Wow.

I used the word WOW a lot during my 63 days. It's such a simple word and easy for my brain to remember when I get tired, but it always totally encapsulated what I was seeing and how I was feeling about what I was seeing.

The magnificence of a mountain is something I never get tired of. It can be in the Highlands of Scotland, in the jungle of Peru, in the desert of Namibia. These large explosions of earth that tower in the skyline make me feel small and yet strong. Their wildness, ruggedness and toughness protrude from the earth and yet there is beauty, serenity and a majestic awe about them.

Ben Nevis dominated the skyline of my day, and I thoroughly loved it. As my day got tougher, I had something to look up at, focus on, breath in and remember just how lucky I was that I was here, seeing this site and doing the thing that I loved.

We had been extremely lucky with the weather we'd faced up to this point. A bit of drizzle here and there, but it had been warm.

Today was the day I was going to test out my new wet weather gear in full. The fog of the morning had cleared and revealed a bright blue sky with white fluffy clouds that rolled over the mountains. However, later in the afternoon, those white fluffy clouds were being chased by dark grey menacing clouds and as I ran, I watched this front of rain roll in.

As I made my way up the right side to the lookout point of Commando Memorial, that dark grey cloud moved in from the left and just as we took our happy snaps at the top of the memorial the weather changed. The wind picked up, the clouds began to burst and light rain became a heavy downpour which became a full-blown hailstorm. Rather than get annoyed at the weather, I was loving it. This was what I'd been expecting from Scotland and although it was wild and extreme, I think I would have been a little disappointed if I'd not experienced a bit of wild and extreme.

Just as quickly as it blew in, the storm blew out and as we were making our way back up Nevis Range to where we'd parked the van earlier that morning the sun came back out again to play.

I secretly love running in crappy weather conditions. It's easy getting out to run during good weather, it takes another level of commitment and determination to persevere when the weather is not so good. It's part of the building of my strength, both physical and mental, it forges my belief that I can get through whatever obstacles are thrown at me.

'I am strong, I will endure. I can achieve what I put my mind to.' are the thoughts that go on loop repeat in my mind.

Prior to starting this adventure, I had mapped out 42.2km routes, but what I foolishly said to Sharif was - let's make them at least 43km routes to ensure that I'd hit my target of a marathon distance each and every day.

Today we took a few extra turns, you could perhaps call them 'wrong turns', I like to call them 'adventuring turns'. Today, I'd 'adventured' quite a way off track and by the time 42.2kms came and went by on my GPS kit, we were still quite a distance from the van.

The only thing to do … keep going.

We did give a little acknowledgement that I had just completed another marathon with a little high five, but rather than start my strip down and cool down routine, I kept shuffling along … a further 2kms.

But honestly what was a couple extra kilometres at the end of the day? Two kilometres is such a little number and so little that I'd probably barely notice it, so Sharif kept telling me as I moaned about just how far away the van was.

At the time I didn't quite see his point of view, but in hindsight he was right, the extra kilometres I'd end up doing either by having to walk to a start location, or shuffle back to an end location when I'd misjudged or gone into 'adventure' mode (i.e., got lost on a route) did become barely noticeable as they became more frequent.

Stan the Van was still playing funny buggers with his electrics. Nothing seemed to be charging and up until this point Sharif hadn't had time to figure out what was going on. We'd talked about this during today's run, the plan was to get to the next location and as I had someone coming to join me for the run, Sharif would spend the day working on the van.

The Scottish poet Robert Burns wrote a poem *To a Mouse* in which the following line 'the best laid plans of mice and men often go awry' has been adapted. Prior to starting this adventure, I had a wonderfully comprehensive plan for my 63 days, but as we were discovering quite early into it, plans don't always go to plan.

We'd arrived in Fort William late in the evening the night before, so we hadn't been able to see the scenery of where we were. Driving out in daylight was such a beautiful sight. I wanted to have a laydown, but the scenery really was too much to miss.

I sat in the front loving what I was seeing, but I was fidgeting and getting irritable and before I knew it, I was in floods of tears.

That plan we'd made of Sharif going home and me continuing on my own was weighing on me. It was two days away and I currently wasn't capable of doing much more than eat, stretch and then pretty much pass out after a marathon.

The tears began not because I was unhappy, they came more at the realisation of the enormity of what I still had to do and what lay ahead of me. Could I really run a marathon every day for 63 days? It was all starting to hit home.

As night closed in, I crawled out of the passenger seat and into the back of the van for a bit of a cry and fitful rest. How was I going to make this happen? How?

Fort William to our next location, Loch Katrine, was a long drive and the lights on the van seemed to be dimming. Sharif called me to come back up front as he was struggling. Cars coming the other way were flicking their lights at us. This was not looking good.

We continued along the windy road until a set of blue lights came up behind us signalling for us to pull over. Sharif steered the van onto the hard shoulder and as we stopped, the engine fully cut out. This was definitely not looking good.

The policeman came up to the van as Sharif wound down the window. Peering in, the officer asked if we had been drinking as we seemed to have forgotten to put our driving lights on. Nope, not the case officer.

The minor nuance with Stan's 'holiday electrics' that we'd been informed of, was proving to be something a little bigger. The van was not only not charging our tech gear, but it also wasn't charging itself and as a result we didn't have any lights nor did we have any charged phones.

Sharif explained what we were doing and where we were going. Thankfully the officer was both understanding and helpful and used his mobile phone to call our recovery service, which also thankfully we'd had the forethought to sign up to before picking up the van.

Apparently, we were on quite a dangerous stretch of road. It was windy, it was narrow and as it was the main road between Fort William and Glasgow, it was well travelled. The policeman said that they would sit behind us with their blues on, the only issue was that the police team that had pulled us over had already had quite an eventful night and were heading back to the police station with a felon in the back of the car.

They waited until another team were able to pull up and babysit us on the side of the road. We were again tag-teamed as this police team went off duty for the night and the next one came in for the midnight to dawn shift.

In the wee small hours of the morning, the recovery truck turned up and hooked us up.

Turns out we were only five kilometres away from the campsite that we had booked, but it had taken us more than 3 hours to get there. We did joke that even I was capable of running faster than this … just.

The final police team that had babysat us knew the owners of the campsite and had forewarned them we would be coming in very late. Unfortunately for our campsite neighbours, not only were we very late, but we were very noisy. The tow truck took us into the site, then backed us up with all its lights shining and its warning beeps beeping. I was going to have a lot of apologising to do in the morning, which was coming around pretty darn quick.

As funny as it was, and we did manage a few laughs throughout the night, and as kind as the police and the recovery truck guy had been, this was not a good night. I was hungry, tired, emotional. I should have passed out, instead I tossed and turned and worried about sleeping in.

As a result, I barely slept a wink.

DAY 6.   LOCH KATRINE, PERTHSHIRE

Friday 1st September, 2017

Daily distance: 43.0km

Time taken: 5hrs 23mins

Total adventure distance: 256.6km

The original planned route was to run along the banks of Loch Katrine, an undulating course which was a short drive away from the campsite. However, we knew for a fact that Stan was not going to be making that drive. The police who'd escorted us to the campsite the night before had mentioned that there was an old railway path at the end of the campsite that could be a good place to run after such an eventful night.

A local runner had booked in to run marathon six with me and due to our lack of charged phones, we had been unable to make contact to explain the predicaments we'd had the night before.

Julie McLean turned up at the campsite bright and shiny and ready to run at the time we'd agreed. Meanwhile I was lolloping about trying to get my body moving, my head focussed, getting as much food as I could get into my belly and I was giving this new suggested route some thought.

I mentioned the suggested route to Julie, but she was still keen to run Loch Katrine, promising me it would be worth the effort. She offered to drive me there so that Sharif could get to the local garage and get Stan on the mend.

Okay. Okay. I was only passing through this way once on this adventure. We were heading to Loch Katrine.

Whilst driving us to today's start location, Julie took it upon her-self to teach me how to say Loch Katrine properly. Apparently, I wasn't.

Having an Aussie accent, I put an Aussie drawl through the middle of a word and then a high inflection as if asking a question at the end of the word and so I was pronouncing the location as Lock Katreeeen? Julie on the other hand, with her Scottish accent, which is an accent I love, I think it sounds quite sing-songish, any-ways she pronounced it as Lohhhhch Ka Trin.

Any which way you pronounce it, Loch Katrine was definitely worth the effort as Julie had said.

It was gorgeous and after yesterday's fog, sun, rain, hail, rain, sun day, the weather today was back to being unseasonably hot for Scotland. I actually stripped down to just my running vest and shorts.

The route was an out and back and Julie said there was a café at the turning point. Not only was there a café, but it was also a café that sold ice-cream. I was definitely ready for ice-cream.

Julie mentioned that she had been a little hesitant in joining me for today's run. She was worried that she'd feel a bit intimidated by someone who had run so many marathons in a row. I quickly pointed out that not only was she running faster than me today, but her marathon times were also faster than even my best time. I was definitely not someone to be intimidated by.

As this was her local area, I asked about the hills and mountains that were surrounding us. Julie explained to me about the practice of 'bagging Munros'. She explained that a Scottish mountain with a height over 3,000 feet (914.4 m) is defined as a Munro - of which there are 282 of them to ascend. Oh, and that she had in fact 'bagged' them all. Wow, what an achievement, she should defi-nitely not be intimidated by me.

Strange how we often worry and compare ourselves with others, and this worry can often lead to intimidation, procrastination, or even worse it can impact on our self-esteem, self-belief and self-confidence.

Sure, look at what someone else has done and cheer their accomplishment, but don't put them on a pedestal that causes feelings of intimidation and unworthiness within yourself. Instead use it as a source of inspiration. Think 'If they can make that possible, what can I do?' - use it to fuel yourself, not put yourself down.

Back to bagging Munros. I was loving hearing Julie's stories of her adventures on the Scottish mountains. This was sounding just like the kind of adventure that I'd like to take on one day and whilst I was listening, I was also mentally adding bagging Munros to my list of 'Adventure To Do's'.

The conversation, the weather, the scenery and the ice-cream were helping me to forget that I'd not had much sleep the previous night. In fact, it was one of the fastest marathons I ran.

This Loch was quite magical. The cruise boat the SS Sir Walter Scott is harboured at the entrance of the Loch. The boat weaves in between several small islands until the Loch opens to a wide expanse of water and it cruises to the café at the far end.

The Loch is surrounded by the hills and mountains of the Trossachs. I had spent a bit of time at the neighbouring Loch Lomond when I was younger with my Grandma, Aunt, Uncle and my cousins. Although this was a new part of the Trossachs, it had a familiarity to it. I was getting closer to the area my family was from.

And that word WOW - I kept saying it over and over again today.

We were making our way back to the start of the Loch when I saw a familiar silhouette in the distance. Sharif was walking the path towards us.

He hadn't been there long enough to see all of the Loch, but what he had seen made him say the sentence that he was repeating over and over again 'Can we come back here when you're not doing something stooopid?'.

This was a place I definitely wanted to come back to, but chances are we'd be back here doing something stooopid, the seed had been sown - bagging Munros had been firmly set in my head as a thing I would do, though I wasn't sure exactly when. Running around, across and through countries is currently my thang. Perhaps bagging Munros would be a brilliant 60th birthday present to myself.

I will be back Loch Katrine. I will be back.

Prior to the drive between Fort William and Loch Katrine we'd been toying with the idea of going back to Nottingham and coming up with a different plan to complete the 63 marathons. We just hadn't quite worked the logistics of it.

Sharif had had some luck with Stan. The guys at the garage had found a loose electric connection between the engine and the battery, explaining the loss of power. They'd managed a quick fix due to the time we had available but had suggested it be looked at properly.

We knew there was no way I'd be able to drive Stan the distances I'd originally planned at the end of each day. Stan needed more mechanical work to be able to keep going. Sharif had to go back to Nottingham to go back to work, we were already struggling with financing this adventure, we couldn't afford for him to take any time off without pay and we'd already earmarked a couple more weeks in which he'd use the rest of his annual leave to go on the road with me.

Although extremely inconvenient, perhaps Stan breaking down was a bit of blessing in disguise.

However, we weren't going home just yet. We had one more marathon planned for Scotland and my cousin, Billy Copeland, had offered to put us up and feed us – an offer way too good to refuse especially after the drama that had occurred the previous night.

Did I mention that I hardly got any sleep, and that I hadn't eaten much, and that I'd run a pretty fast marathon? I may have mentioned it more than once, twice, or a gazillion times to Sharif when I got into the van.

I definitely suffer from 'hangry' syndrome: a hunger + anger combination. Whilst I'd been running, Sharif had been to the supermarket and had the solution, all he had to do was put up with me for the drive to Glasgow. We got to Billy's house, went straight into the kitchen and before I could say where's the shower – Sharif had seared a great big, fat, juicy, practically-covering-the-entire-dinner-plate, steak.

An abundance of good food and a comfy bed was just what I needed, and I crashed.

Thankfully Sharif was in a better physical place than me and he got to know my relatives through the night, my family reunion would have to wait until the morning.

DAY 7.   GLASGOW, LANARKSHIRE

Saturday 2nd September, 2017

Daily distance: 42.7km

Time taken: 7hrs 4mins

Total adventure distance: 299.3km

The original plans for my time in Glasgow had been to run partway along the West Highland Way, but whilst I was pretty much passed out in bed, Sharif and Billy's son, Taylor, had spent the night looking at maps.

Rather than drive to Milngavie, which again I was told I had pronounced completely wrong – I mean how can you get the word Mull-guy, which is the Scottish pronunciation, from Milngavie which has both an N and a V slotted in there? It spells Miln Gavie doesn't it?

I digress.

Rather than drive to Milngavie, Taylor pointed out that the Strathclyde canal was just outside and at the end of their road, and that I could run along that path and just see where my feet would take me. It was flat, it was pretty, it would take me through Glasgow, and it went for a very long way which meant I could just keep running along it until I reached my required distance for the day.

As part of this adventure I had wanted to visit iconic British locations which the West Highland Way would have ticked, but I had also wanted it to be a personal tour of the places that meant something to me, and as Glasgow was the birthplace of both of my parents, the opportunity to get a good feel for this city and run along the canal was an opportunity too good to miss – and did I mention that it was flat?

Sharif showed me the change of plans in the morning and I was on board.

Bill decided to join me for the start of my run. Bill doesn't run and his wife Dympna and his kids, Taylor and Ashleigh, thought this was an hilarious turn of events. It was.

Suited and booted for his day at work, he lined up with me as I set my watches and trackers. As I took off, he took off with me. A hundred metres in and he was puffing and panting and suggesting I slow the pace down. Yes, he was unfit, but his lack of breath was due mainly to all the laughing – Bill was laughing, Taylor and Ashleigh were in hysterics and he just couldn't catch his breath. He suggested he leave the running to me and waved me off on my day.

As I ran along the Clydesdale I reflected on my past and my family. Glasgow was where my parents, Robert and Vivien had both been born and had grown up. They met at the tender age of 15 at the local ice-skating rink. Rob was a speed skater and Viv was a figure skater, two very different disciplines, but that didn't stop them falling in love. They had been very keen to leave Glasgow. Rob was first to go when he received a fitter and turner's apprenticeship based in England. He moved and set up residence in Rochdale with the other apprenticeship lads whilst Viv remained in Glasgow working as a hairdresser. They courted long distance for four years until they married, at which point Viv moved to Rochdale, and a couple of years later they popped me out into the world.

Whilst they had left Glasgow, they were still in the UK and they still had itchy feet. Shortly after my first birthday they emigrated by boat to Australia.

As I ran through Glasgow, I wondered why they had been so keen to leave this city. However, having thought that, I realised that I had also been very keen to leave my own hometown of Geelong, Australia.

It wasn't that I didn't like it, Geelong is actually a very beautiful city. It's just that I loved looking at maps, atlases and globes that showed this whole entire world. A world that, as a kid, I longed to discover and experience. To me the whole world that was painted on my globe was my home. I didn't quite understand the realities of borders or of cultural differences that would have meant as a woman I'd have less freedom to move about, to learn, and to experience life. I just always imagined that I'd be able to roam the world.

This was another of one of my whys — a deep, personal reason. I wanted to see the world, and I was beginning to believe that perhaps I could run the world. I was formulating a bit of a plan and this was a training adventure to see if I could make this idea a reality.

Whilst the 63 marathons in 63 days was a huge adventurous challenge of its own, I was also seeing it as a stepping-stone, as were all the previous runs, adventures and experiences I had gone through. They were all about building the person that I am today and who I will become tomorrow. I was strong. Stronger than I ever thought possible and I was making this dream come true, so what else was I capable of? Was I strong enough to run around the world one day? I now knew that this was something I wanted to find out.

I ran, looking at the world I was passing through. I read the historical signs about the canal I was running along. I took in the beauty of the water and the surrounding land.

I posted messages back to my parents thanking them for showing me how to be brave and ambitious and to chase after your dreams. They had done it by moving to Australia. They didn't quite understand why I had chosen to return to the UK, but they did understand the urge to want to expand and push myself.

I ran alone along the canal whilst Sharif made plans for our end of day. We'd made a decision about the adventure logistics. After I'd finished today's marathon and had some food and a shower back at Billy's, we were going to head back to Nottingham together in Stan, leaving the car that we'd originally driven up in, there in Glasgow.

How we would get the car home was put on the 'To Do' list for later thought. For now, I just had to concentrate on finishing marathon number seven, Sharif had to plan the long drive home, and together we'd discuss week two which I now had no idea about or how it was going to look.

In my mind, the best way to deal with the uncertainty was to not think too deeply about it and rather like today's run, simply set off in a direction, roll with it and see where my feet would take me.

It was actually a great tactic to deal with the enormity of this adventure. Rather than think about the fact that I had eight weeks left and that I hadn't planned any routes for the following day or week, all I thought about was the timeframe I was in. The kilometre that I was running in my current 5km block. I was still following my run 5km, eat, stretch, drink then get going on the next 5km routine. I ran, I looked up and I looked around at the beauty that was right here and immediately around me.

Whilst Sharif was sorting the car and the van, he was also keeping tabs on me and calculated that I'd finish at the Falkirk Wheel, an amazing piece of engineering that lifts boats from one canal, Forth and Clyde, and places it on another, Union Canal. He headed to my finish line, parked up and started back along the canal on Scotty to meet me and keep me company as I finished off my day.

The mini new plan was going well. I'd finished my marathon, we'd returned to Billy's, we'd eaten, I'd showered, and we'd set off in Stan. Next stop: Nottingham.

We drove off into the fading daylight, and all was going well until it wasn't.

As the darkness rolled in, the van headlights began to fade again. We needed to pull off the motorway and make some adjustments.

A bit of luck. A sign. A truck stop was just up here. Just a little bit further ... along this slip road ... just a little ...

Ahhhhhh.

Nope.

Oh Stan, you really were being a naughty van.

On the upside, and it is always important to find an upside, we had charged mobiles this time so not quite as bad as the first time, but we weren't home. Maybe Stan was having second thoughts on leaving his home country of Scotland? All we knew was that we were just shy of the Scottish/English border and had only driven 100 miles out of a 300-mile road trip.

We called recovery again and waited. When the guy arrived, he advised that the temporary fix just wasn't holding up (we kind of figured that) and recommended that we really should pull over for the night and only drive when we didn't have to use the headlights. Okay, so we had a solution, albeit not a great one, but it was going to have to do for now.

He jump-started the van and we made it to the truck stop. This was going to be a long night.

Sharif set the alarm for 5:30am, not that we needed an alarm, the noise of trucks coming and going went on all night. Morning came around way too quickly and bleary eyed, I headed into the truck shop/café for some much-needed caffeine.

Cold sausage rolls and pasties seem to be the 'go to' food in the trucking world. As I was starving and tired, I grabbed a selection and figured that it was going to have to do until we reached a highway services with something a bit more appealing.

We only had a six-hour drive home before I could start my second week and get over my next mental milestone - marathon number eight. Thankfully it was a beautiful drive.

Enter the unknown
With knowledge bred of your past
To forge new normal

~ Nikki Love

WEEK 2

DAY 8. GAMSTON, NOTTINGHAMSHIRE

Sunday 3rd September, 2017

Daily distance: 42.8km

Time taken: 5hrs 55mins

Total adventure distance: 342.1km

We arrived back in Nottingham at around 12 noon and I've got to say, the travel, the lack of sleep, the not so healthy food all combined was making me feel a bit woozy and wobbly.

I was dressed to run, but I needed a little nap. Just a little laydown.

I didn't even make it up to my bed.

'Sharif, can you wake me in an hour' I slurred.

I lay on the sofa and drifted off.

I woke with a jolt.

I had a marathon to run.

I had to get my senses together.

I put my shoes on. Set my watches, GPS and tracker and stumbled out the door.

My tummy did not feel good, but I realised that I was on day 8 and I was feeling better than I had that very first time I'd run a multi-day event. At the end of my 7in7 adventure I had gone to bed shattered and on that eighth day I woke up and could barely move. I crawled from my bed to the kitchen to get some food, I then staggered back to my bed and that's pretty much where I stayed for the entire day. On that eighth day my body was in agony from head to toe.

I wasn't feeling on top of the world after the past 24 hours' she-nanigans, but my body felt capable of running and I knew that I was going to go out there and do my best to be my best and get through the day.

At least my route was familiar. I had a loop that I'd been training on as part of the preparation for this adventure. It was a simple out and back along the Grantham canal, this would get me through the first 12kms.

Back home from that first loop, Sharif mentioned that I looked pretty pale. My tummy really did not feel good.

As I headed off in a different direction but another of my familiar training loops, around Colwick Park, Sharif hopped on the bike and rode alongside me.

Just keep putting one foot in front of the other was the chant inside my head.

Sharif had called friends to see if anyone was about who could join me for the second half of my day.

Just keep putting one foot in front of the other.

My friend, Arwen Makin said she'd join me for a bit. We were going to be running past her house, so we'd pick her up shortly. Arwen messaged Sharif several times asking if she'd missed us. Nope, I was just taking slow and steady to a whole new level.

Finally arriving at Arwen's, she offered to take the lead in navigating where to run. Holme Pierrepont Country Park, another of my local running haunts, was nearby but she was keen to show me a wilder route around the man-made rowing lake rather than the usual tarmacked path that most people run along, I was all up for that. Quite a lot had happened since we last saw Arwen and she wanted to know everything. I wasn't capable of talking much, but Sharif was, so I let them chatter away whilst I listened and shuffled.

'Nic, you really don't look too good', Arwen said as I took a breather.

'I'm okay', I responded. 'Oh. No. Hold on. Just need to find a bush. Back in a min'.

… and out it came.

Oky doky then, I thought as I wiped the sweat from my brow and the puke from mouth, perhaps now that I'd expunged this stomach queasiness, I might feel a little bit better.

Ooops, no. The other end. Thank goodness for the bush cover.

'Are you alright?' both Arwen and Sharif shouted over.

I was sweating, stuff was coming out of each end. I had half a marathon to run.

Was I alright? No, not really.

Was I going to get through this? Yes, I was going to find a way.

I stayed behind the bushes checking in with myself - was I ready to go? Yep, I think my insides were empty for now. Thank goodness Arwen had decided to show me the wilder side of Holme Pierrepont. And thankfully I had learned much about having to 'go' in the middle of nowhere, and what I should carry, from when I had run through the Peruvian jungle. Toilet paper, doggy poo bags, and antibacterial hand gel go everywhere with me when I run. It's why you'll always see me wearing some form of backpack. I was well prepared for this eventuality.

I finally emerged from my little area of urban jungle, wiped the tears away from my eyes and I settled back into a shuffle alongside Arwen and Sharif.

We dropped Arwen back home and then it was back to just me shuffling and Sharif on the bike.

Just keep putting one foot in front of the other.

Night was rolling in. I was nearly there, but I still had that last little bit to finish. I was now running along the footpaths around my house, circling around and around.

I think this was possibly some of the toughest circling I did throughout the 63 days.

I was at home. I just wanted to get inside and sleep. It took everything I had to keep going to make sure my watches and my GPS had all hit the 42.2km mark.

One of the reasons I had chosen 63 locations away from my home was that I'd previously experienced this feeling of being so close to home but not finished. On day four of my 7in7, I had been driven out to a start location and from there I then ran back to my house. Unfortunately, I misjudged the distance, and I reached my house without reaching the 42.2kms target, falling short by a couple of kilometres. I was in pain, which was exacerbated tenfold by having to run past my home.

I had not wanted to repeat that experience during my 63 marathons adventure, I wasn't sure that I'd have the mental strength to be so close to home and still keep going.

However, that was exactly what I was doing now, and for the next few days at least I was going to be at home, so I knew I had to change my perspective on that past experience and change it fast.

That day in 2010, I did run past my house. I cried possibly every step of the final kilometres until I made it back to my house. I remembered that I did not enjoy it one little bit, but I had to find those positives.

I remembered that I never gave up. I remembered that I had proven to myself that I was strong both physically and mentally. I had learned that I was capable of more than I thought, and here I was, seven years on, doing it again and although I'd been sick throughout the day, I was still running.

Maybe I was strong enough to cope with being around my house.

Throughout the second half of my day I was thinking of all the benefits I'd have by being at home. I could do loops and return home to eat at the end of each loop. This also meant toilet facilities – and my tummy was still grumbling.

If I wanted this adventure to continue, and I wanted it as much as I wanted to breathe, then I had to believe I could.

I was strong.

I was capable.

I was adaptable.

I finished!

DAY 9. GAMSTON TO ROTHLEY, LEICESTERSHIRE

Monday 4th September, 2017

Daily distance: 43.2km

Time taken: 6hrs 7mins

Total adventure distance: 385.3km

Sharif was trying to stay one step ahead of me as we rearranged a running schedule for the time I was going to be back in Nottingham. Today's plan was to run from Nottingham to Leicester, it was a route I knew well, I'd used it as a training run prior to this adventure. There was also an added bonus to this run in that my son Riley would be at the other end.

I hadn't intended on seeing Riley in person until the middle of this adventure as my original location map took me from the north to the south of the country, so getting to see him gave me a boost for day nine.

I had survived yesterday, slept in my own bed, the sickness had gone, and I can honestly say that my legs didn't feel too bad.

Riley was at school during the day, but his dad, Willis, had organised to pick him up, grab his bike and meet me at a village on the outskirts of Leicester. I kept the thought of seeing Riley in my head as I set off.

Whilst I had done this route before, the last time I had cruised along it without giving too much thought to the places I was running past, or my history with them.

Being in the state I was in today, tired and a bit run down from the expungement of bodily fluids yesterday, my emotion levels were running high and this route was triggering some old emotions. I figured the best thing I could do was think about my past experiences with kindness, as they were the things that had shaped me into the person that I was today, and I was pretty proud that this person was here chasing her dreams, her goals and her ambitions.

The first blast from my past was running along the River Trent towards the village of Wilford. I'd run this stretch so many times during the training for my second marathon.

It being my 'second' marathon is significant. My first marathon attempt had ended in a DNF, which for any non-runners reading this stands for Did Not Finish, not really the target result for a running race.

Riley was only 6 months old when I entered the Nottingham Marathon on a bit of a whim after a sickly pregnancy. I'd suffered with hyperemesis gravidarum during my pregnancy which basically meant I threw up a lot and I'd had to stay in hospital several times throughout Riley's nine months incubation to be put on a drip because I couldn't keep food or liquids down. The sickness started at six weeks and lasted until I pushed that big, beautiful head out and into the world.

I loved being a mum, and I loved my baby boy, but I was desperate to run again. Despite all of my marathon ambitions, I don't really recall doing any runs longer than 5kms in the lead up to that first marathon. This could have explained the result that ensued.

At the 19 miles sign, I stopped. I thought I had nothing left to give and I gave up.

I went home, looked into my baby's big brown eyes and realised that 'I gave up' was not the story I wanted to tell him. It was a fact, but I wanted it to be a part of a longer story in which I'd tell him that I'd started, got knocked down, got back up again and eventually succeeded.

I wanted to be a marathon runner and by golly I was going to become a marathon runner, so I entered the London marathon which was six months later (once upon a time, you could enter the London marathon and pretty much be guaranteed a place, nowadays it's about a one in twenty chance). I trained with purpose and commitment along this stretch of the River Trent, and as I ran it today, I remembered back with pride at how strong I had been to keep going in the face of failure. A lesson that had shaped me for this current run.

Just to let you know, I completed the 2002 London Marathon just under my target time of 5 hours. I breezed it home in 4:59:38.

Next blast from my past along today's route was my old house in Ruddington. So many memories here with so many connections to where I was today.

Firstly, how we'd bought the house.

Willis and I bought the house shortly after Riley was born, from one of his best mates, Dirk ... and this seems a fitting time for me to further introduce you to Dirk.

As I mentioned, I was doing this run to make good a promise I'd made to him after he was diagnosed with the hereditary disease Huntington's.

Dirk was in his late thirties when he was told that his dad had passed away. His dad had died as an unidentified person, and the ensuing autopsy had revealed that he had been afflicted with Huntington's.

Dirk decided to get tested and discovered that he too had Huntington's Disease. I have written more about the disease at the end of the book, the symptoms that show and the decline that people go through with this horrible disease that currently has no cure. When you get to the end, please do read.

Willis and I bought our house from Dirk prior to his diagnosis. He had been looking to sell and we had been looking to buy in the countryside now that we had a baby. Unfortunately for me and Willis as a couple with a new baby, a new house, a new business and a new dynamic to our lives, our relationship was straining. Three months after buying the Ruddington house we started to part.

I often think back on that time and wonder how I managed to get through it. I had no family in this country. I had no friends outside of Willis' circle. I had a 12-month-old beautiful baby. I had a fledgling business. That first twelve months of separation was tough.

I had used training for the London marathon as a handy diversion from my personal life, but once that was complete, I struggled. I struggled to sleep, to focus, I cried … a lot.

I'd started to build a circle of friends with some of the mothers in the village who were being very supportive, but they were also concerned about my personal mental state and this came to a head when one of the mums saw me parked up, asleep in my car with Riley asleep in his car seat.

I had been spending my days driving around in the village to get Riley to sleep. Once he was asleep, I would pull over, cry my eyes out and fall asleep too.

My friends suggested I go and see a doctor, as I was struggling. I'd been so worried about telling people I wasn't coping. I was even more worried that, if I told a doctor, they would take Riley away, citing I was unfit to care for him. My head was constantly racing that I was going to lose my house, my baby, my everything. I finally gave in, booked a doctor's appointment and instead of taking me away or my baby away, I was prescribed anti-depressants.

I began sleeping better, feeling calmer, and I was able to think more rationally. These fears I had about losing everything still played in my head, but I was thinking them through better. I had to re-find my strengths. I also realised that I had stopped running.

Running helped me think, it helped me feel good. How had I lost it?

As the medication kicked in and my thought processes became more rational, I'm talking about ten days, I remembered that I was in charge of the way I felt and the actions that I took.

I bought a running buggy. I got rid of the pills. I left the car at home. I ran with my baby. I got stronger physically and mentally.

Wow. This stuff was pouring back as I ran past my old Ruddington house, along the streets and through the country park that I had pushed Riley's running buggy and where I'd taught him to walk and play and run, as he grew.

As I ran, I remembered how strong I was, I remembered what I was capable of enduring and I knew what I was striving for, I thought about Dirk and the fight he was going through, I knew all the reasons Why I was going to get through these 63 marathons.

I knew it.

So far, I'd felt aches and pains from running, but as I continued on day nine, I noticed there was a bit more of a strain in my right thigh.

One of my assets leading into this adventure was my professional background. I was a sports massage therapist and personal trainer. I'd spent years looking after people's aches, pains and injuries. My expertise was not only in dealing with the issue, but also finding the source of the problem through assessing a person's body movement and mechanics. Most commonly, issues arose due to weaknesses, imbalances and repetitive body movement.

Today I was running along a road with quite a camber which meant my right leg was on a bit of road that was sloping down to the right. There was a lot of imbalance and repetitive body movement going on today. I hadn't really noticed this side-of-road slope the last time I'd ran this route, but the last time that I'd ran it, I was doing it on fresh legs.

I'm often asked about injury and how I coped.

As this was my first multi-week adventure, I was not sure how my body was going to cope. Upon reflection, having done a few more multi-weeks adventures and having spoken to other runners who've pushed the multi-week boundaries, I've realised that there is a similar pattern to what our body goes through. I was currently in the running phase which I now refer to as the terrible twos.

Here's my take on what happens to your body on these multi-week adventures.

The first week of an adventure and your body moves along okay, everything seems to be in working order, the adventure is all bright and shiny and new.

The second week and your body starts to talk back to you 'hey, hold on a minute sunshine, this is ridiculous' and it starts throwing little tantrums – the terrible two's. You feel more aches, more pains, and you wonder if your body is ever going to get used to the strain you are putting it under.

By week three, it's like your body says 'oh, so you're still doing this, oky doky then, I may as well join you'.

By week four the repetition becomes the norm, and a new habit has been formed. Your body likes to operate in a state of homeostasis and eventually settles into the new normal that you've created.

I was currently in week two and today I had to deal with a terrible two's leg tantrum.

I wasn't going to stop doing the thing that was hurting, which would have been my suggestion as a therapist. Instead I had to change the prevailing repetitively straining conditions ... I had to cross over and run on the other side of the road.

It's common practice when road running to run into the on-coming traffic, that way you can see and take aversive actions to cars that don't like sharing the road with runners. Thankfully, the route I was running along was quiet country backroads, so I was able to drift from side to side without putting myself or any car drivers at risk.

After a roller-coaster emotional morning I made it to the village where I was meeting Riley. I hadn't seen him in about ten days. Had he grown? I think he had. Oh, my heart. I love this kid so much.

Riley will always be one of my biggest personal WHYs for the things I do.

As well as proving to myself that I can do the things that I set my mind to, he sees me doing it and I think, and hope, that he is learning from me. At some point he will face obstacles, experience heartbreak, feel overwhelmed. If he knows that he is loved, that he is strong, that he can do anything he puts his mind to, then I will have taught, shared, and done everything I could do as a mum.

From the point Riley joined me, we had just 7kms to reach today's end. We chatted about his days since I last saw him, how he was getting on at school and he moaned that I was running so slowly that he was nearly falling off his bike. I loved every minute of it.

Today's end was perfect, my watches and GPS gear all clicked over the 42.2kms about a kilometre away from a pub that had been my local when I lived in Leicester, and the place that had I originally met Sharif. I shuffled on with Riley riding alongside me as I called Sharif and Willis to meet us at this 'perfect' rendezvous point.

Just a little sidenote, way back in 2002/3 when Willis and I split, we had a lot of emotions to go through and get over. What we both acknowledged was that we had started our relationship as friends and that 'friends' status was something that we both wanted to get back to. We both loved Riley with all our hearts, we both wanted to be the best parents we could be and being friends made raising Riley together apart so much easier.

I sat in the pub with these three guys in my life, Sharif, Willis and Riley and we had a little cheer to the end of day nine. I was proud of where I'd come, where I was going, who I had around me and I was one very happy gal.

DAY 10. BEESTON CANAL, NOTTINGHAMSHIRE

Tuesday 5th September, 2017

Daily distance: 42.8km

Time taken: 5hrs 58mins

Total adventure distance: 428.1km

I had a massage booked for the end of the day, which was a lovely reward to look forward to, the cost of gaining the reward was to get through marathon ten.

Sharif and I had spent the previous night looking at local routes and formulating new plans whilst we were waiting for Stan to be fixed. I was going to use the Grantham canal as my 'wake up' loop.

The Grantham canal was straight out my front door, a climb over a short fence and I was on the canal path. I could make the loop as long or as short as I liked, the canal from my house went all the way to Grantham which was twenty-six miles away.

The first loop, however long I chose it to be, allowed me to eat, wake up (which is exactly how the order of events felt every morning - I'd eat with my eyes closed drifting somewhere in between sleeping and consciousness), run, get back home again, use the toilet facilities, eat again and then set off for the remainder of my day.

My first loop was also going to be my 'take Rufus for a run' loop. As well as seeing Riley during yesterday's run, we also popped into my friends, Ben and Tamsin Robinson, who had been kindly looking after my pooch, Rufus, whilst we'd been off galivanting throughout the country.

Rufus was my little girl, my training partner, my reason for running on days that I didn't really feel like it. One mention of the word 'run', and she would bound around the lounge, giving sweet little yelps to get me to move faster and let her out onto the canal path. Rufus loves running more than I do.

After the first loop, I'd then head in the opposite direction which was towards the River Trent either turning left at the river for a long out and back to complete the distance or a turn right at the river to do a figure eight around two of my favourite training haunts, Colwick Park and Holme Pierrepont.

Today's turn at the river was left and the goal was to get to the Attenborough Nature Reserve, this direction also took me by Sharif's place of work.

Despite having my dog as company on my first loop, the grey, wet weather was getting a little inside my head. As I called into Sharif's work, I had a little cry and a moan on his shoulder blubbing that running around Nottingham was not exactly the vision of adventure that I'd had for this challenge.

Sharif listened, nodded, gave me a little cuddle then told me to jog on. This was now his main job, you know, as well as earn a living, make my coffee and breakfast and packed lunch (and usually my dinner), he was also there to hear me out, provide me with a comforting shoulder, but then push me off out the door, reminding me of the bigger picture of what I was trying to achieve. And so, I wiped away my tears on his shirt and ran on.

Attenborough Nature Reserve is a beautiful, serene space that's listed in the top ten 'eco places in the world' and is usually frequented by an abundance of walkers, ramblers, bird watchers and nature enthusiasts. However, we had been experiencing some funny old weather patterns and while it was a relatively warm day, it was also raining, resulting in sticky humid conditions.

Perhaps the weather was keeping people away, or perhaps it was because it was a weekday and most people were at work and not running stooopid crazy distances, any which way, it felt like I had this entire space mostly to myself.

I genuinely love running around in nature, but within a reserve, it's like the sounds of nature are tuned in and turned up to full volume. As I ran, I immersed myself in the sounds and sights of this beautiful piece of world - the movement of the trees as the wind and the rain passed through, the chirpings of the birds that I could see as well as those I could only hear, the rustle in the undergrowth as the wildlife moved about its daily life, the flight of the bumblebees and dragonflies as they flitted and buzzed around and about me.

The time and distance flew by as I shuffled my way around the nature reserve, it was only on my way back home along the river that I noticed the drab weather conditions again and remembered my sore and achy thigh from yesterday's run. Thankfully there were quite a few shops along the River Trent that stocked ice-creams and having an ice-cream or two was just what the doctor (well my head) ordered, to take my mind off the weather and said sore and achy thigh.

Later that evening, after eating all the food in sight and immersing my achy thigh into an Epsom salt bath, my sports therapist, Clare Riddell, popped in to attend to my legs. Clare had been my tutor whilst I was learning sports massage therapy way back in 2010, which was also the year of my 7in7, so she was experienced in how to deal with my aches, pains and crazy ideas. Her verdict was 'you're in much better shape than I thought you'd be' and after ten days of running my little socks off, I was very happy with her professional opinion.

Onwards.

DAY 11. GRANTHAM CANAL, NOTTINGHAMSHIRE

Wednesday 6th September, 2017

Daily distance: 42.4km

Time taken: 7hrs 18mins

Total adventure distance: 470.5km

I wouldn't say that day eleven was the day that the wheels fell off my bus, but it was the first day that my belly didn't follow my plan of run a 'wake up' loop and get home to use the toilet facilities.

I mentioned that one of the most commonly asked questions asked of my running adventures is 'where did I go to the toilet?' and my rehearsed response (because I talk to school children and this seems like the best phrase to use) is that when there are no toilets around and I'm in the middle of nowhere, I jungle poo.

Well I was less than two kilometres away from home, my tummy rumbled and there was not a jungle to be seen. No, no, no, noooooo …

Prior to this adventure, I would often tell a story to people I was coaching about the importance of being able to 'kick' at the end of a race. Being able to kick at the end of a race is the ability to find another gear and push as hard as you can to finish your race either faster than your previous best time or, as I describe in the story, faster than someone who has had a bad day running.

Let me enlighten you.

Way back in 2010 on the final run of my 7in7 I had quite an experience.

As I was heading down the last 400 yards of the London marathon – the bit just before the bend which leads to the homestretch where all the cameras are waiting to capture the ecstasy and agony of the faces of the men and women who think that running 26.2 miles and pushing their bodies to extremes that they often never thought possible is just the best way to spend a Sunday (I truly believe it is by the way, but apparently there are people out there who think that's just insane) …

Anyway, back to the story …

As I reached the last 400 yards, knowing that the end of my seventh marathons was nigh, I shuffled on with a little more speed and I ran up alongside a gent who looked like he was having a bad day. He was wearing yellow lycra shorts, which he probably regretted at this point of the day, and his yellow lycra shorts unfortunately showed that his tummy had not played nice. He'd pooped his pants.

Whilst feeling very sorry for the dude with poopy pants, and I'm sure he was a lovely fellow, I was pretty darn adamant that I hadn't just run the best part of 7 marathons in 7 days to be photographed next to him and his bad day shorts. I remembered the training tactic 'kick'.

I was knackered, I was in pain, but somehow, from somewhere deep down inside, I found the energy to kick. I said 'Well done, see ya later' to Mr Poopy Pants and blasted away and down the homestretch towards those happy snapping sports photographers.

Little did I know that I should have taken pride in the fact that I had never once pooped my pants through running. Unfortunately, it is now an accolade that I can't boast about. However, I have learned my lesson to take pride in the circumstances that you are currently in, because they may change. I can now proudly boast that I can still count the number of times that I have pooped my pants on my hands. Now for all you non-runners reading this, you may be wondering 'Well what's the boast in that?'. Well, I haven't had to use my tootsies as my abacas to count how many times I have pooped my running pants as yet and unfortunately, knowing what I know now about ultrarunning, I think it's probably only a matter of time.

As for the right now, I had one of those realisations 'Oh my golly, I was now Mr Poopy Pants.'

Thankfully, I was close to home and I didn't have to finish my marathon in this state. I went inside, cleaned and showered myself, shed a little tear whilst popping on a change of clothes and headed back out the door.

This really was the highlight of the day. I stayed close to home repeating this canal loop throughout the day, more tears fell from my eyes until marathon eleven was complete.

DAY 12. THRUMPTON, NOTTINGHAMSHIRE

Thursday 7th September, 2017

Daily distance: 42.7km

Time taken: 5hrs 59mins

Total adventure distance: 513.2km

The intense emotions, my dodgy tummy, the diarrhoea, ahhhhh, it all made sense. Throughout the night my period started, and these symptoms were all associated with this time of my cycle. However, as well as being menstrual, I am also in the weird and not-so-wonderful phase of life called the perimenopause. As well as my usual period symptoms, I was also sweating more (hot flushes), and I had started experiencing brain fogginess. Mainly it was an inability to think fast and clear and make rational decisions, especially when under duress, and running 63 marathons in a row was a fair bit of duress.

When I was preparing myself for my running adventures, I researched people who had done long distances over long periods of time, I was curious how other women handled their menstrual cycle and how they navigated their way through the perimenopausal phase of their lives. Mostly, the books of inspiration I had read were by men, and the few women's books I read didn't really broach either subject.

I figured I was just going to have to work this one out myself, but I also promised that if I did write a book, I would write about my experience.

Here's what I learned … it's annoying having your period during a long-distance adventure and during the perimenopausal phase of life it just plain sucks.

I had experienced having my period during one of my shorter long-distance adventures when it started on day four of the JungleUltra, in Peru. I had expected it at some stage, my periods were still coming regularly at this point in my life, so I was carrying tampons and doggy poo bags with me so that I could achieve my commitment to the race code and leave no rubbish behind in the jungle and this included toilet paper and any other sanitary products.

When I talk about my running adventures, I mention that running through the jungle was probably one of the scariest adventures I have ever done. The terrain was often scary with some of the paths that we were traversing along being no wider than the width of my feet and the drops off the sides of the mountains were extremely steep. I also knew there were things in the jungle that could kill me, including snakes, spiders and jaguars, and that caiman lived along the waterways and they too could do a good job of killing me. So, from day four I had the added fear that I was carrying blood soaked sanitary items in the top of my backpack. I was genuinely petrified, but I ran on.

On the positive side of today's run, I was no longer in a jungle and the fear of being tracked down by a ferocious killer animal because I was carrying blood soaked sanitary products was not high, however I still had the issue of having to find regular places to be able to change myself throughout the day.

The goal for today's run had been to run to Loughborough via the River Trent. Not the side of the river that I had run along earlier in the week, but the other side that I knew very little about. It was the side of the river that was wilder with more woodland and fields to run through. This meant it was also quieter, more secluded and had longer distances between villages. This, I soon discovered, meant no shops to buy ice-cream or purchase that other stuff that really helps when you run - water.

It was warm and humid, I was sweating like a sweaty thing, I was bleeding like a bleedy thing and I was struggling to concentrate and follow the right dirt tracks that were my planned route, instead I kept taking paths that led me to dead ends.

I was frustrated, emotional, dehydrated, struggling to focus and stay calm. I called Sharif several times throughout the day moaning about everything - how my body felt, how my head felt, how I kept taking wrong turns and how I couldn't even find a shop in the village that I'd just run through.

I kept running, trying to get to my final destination along the route that had been plotted for me when something finally snapped. It wasn't a jaguar or a caiman, it was a field of cows, but in the state of mind I was in, those cows were probably going to kill me just as badly as any Peruvian wildlife could have.

I called Sharif and asked him to help me plot a route home that took me along quiet roads and back into some civilisation where I could buy an ice-cream, I desperately needed ice-cream ... and water, water would probably do wonders for my hysterical peri-menopausal brain. I about faced, traipsed across several fields until I finally hit tarmac and headed home.

As I ran back into the outskirts of Nottingham, and as if by magic, an ice-cream van pulled up right in front of me. I was going to get through this day, by golly I was.

DAY 13. BEESTON CANAL, NOTTINGHAMSHIRE

Friday 8th September, 2017

Daily distance: 42.6km

Time taken: 5hrs 56mins

Total adventure distance: 555.8km

Today I was being joined by someone I didn't know, a friend of a friend, but by the end of the day Neil Byford would become an amazing friend for life. Neil was a friend of Arwen's from the running club Beeston AC, but they had another common connection, they both raised money for the charity HDA as Neil's dad has Huntington's Disease. Today I was going to run and listen to the story of Neil and his dad, Stuart, and stay on the side of the River Trent that sold ice-creams.

Neil's dad now lives in a nursing home which is providing him with the palliative care he will need for the remainder of his life as he loses more and more control of his body. Again, please read the information about Huntington's at the end of this book to understand more about this disease and why the charity HDA exists.

Neil had visited his dad the night before our run and had told him what I was doing and that we'd be running together, his dad was adamant that he wanted to donate to the charity. Thank you and bless you, Mr Byford.

As well as learning about his dad, I also learned that Neil was a very good runner, and that he would normally finish way ahead of me with the fast crowd. It's hard running 26.2 miles at the best of times, it's even harder for someone who runs at the pace of a hare to slow down and run at the pace of somewhere in between a snail and a tortoise. It's not the distance that is the issue, it's the unusual length of time to be shuffling on their feet, which in to-day's case was just short of 6 hours in the unseasonably warm and humid weather.

As well as Neil, I had Rufus for company too. Having run along this side of the River Trent a few times now, I knew there were plenty of opportunities for her to drink water and to cool herself off in the river and she did love to run. I'd made sure both of my running buddies had been taken care of, I'd carried plenty of food for Rufus and I'd made sure that Neil and I had passed enough shops with ice-creams to help us get through the marathon.

I had no major emotional wobbles, although I did shed quite a few tears about Neil's dad, and I did have to make a dramatic save of my numpty dog, who'd leant a little too far over the river wall (which was the only stretch of the river that she couldn't paddle into). Thankfully I was able to reach down over the wall and fish her out. Numpty dog.

At the end of the day Neil and I reflected on our run. We'd eaten our ice-creams, we'd ran 26.2 miles, I'd received notifications that we'd raised some more money for HDA along the way, there was just one more ultra-marathon-running protocol to follow, and that was to head to the pub for a pint of pale ale.

DAY 14. GRANTHAM CANAL, NOTTINGHAMSHIRE

Saturday 9th September, 2017

Daily distance: 42.5km

Time taken: 5hrs 43mins

Total adventure distance: 598.3km

The end of week two was one of my recovery marathons – yeah, we'd started referring to these home runs as a recovery marathon.

Out and back along the Grantham canal. A pootle out to Holme Pierrepont, around the rowing lake and back, and a final loop back along the canal.

Today was all about getting the distance done and checking in and counting all of my swans and cygnets. I know they weren't my swans, and it wasn't necessarily my job, but I had been counting the swan families and it was heart-breaking when one of the babies went missing (and they often did). I ran and I counted, and I reported back to Sharif that all was well with my canal friends.

I had also made a new real-life friend along my recovery marathon route. I'd started talking to a lovely gent by the name of Peter, or Canal Peter as I referred to him, every day that I ran along the Grantham canal.

Canal Peter walked his daughter's dog, Diesel, every morning along part of my run. Each day he'd check in and ask what number marathon I was on, how I was feeling, he'd tell me I was mad and then he'd give me his low down on the swans and cygnets (I wasn't the only one who had invested their hearts into them). I'd then carry on with a see you tomorrow, or whatever day it was that I was going to be back doing my recovery marathon.

I ran along as the day moved along, and dare I say it ... I think I was getting into the groove of daily marathon running.

A twist, a pivot
What's that ... Opportunity
Hear, see, take, embrace

~ Nikki Love

WEEK 3

DAY 15. RUTLAND WATER, RUTLAND

Sunday 10th September, 2017

Daily distance: 42.3km

Time taken: 6hrs 12mins

Total adventure distance: 640.6km

I was heading into week three, and to tell the truth I was quite amazed about how I was feeling and that I was still going. As I mentioned, my body was starting to get used to the daily routine of running a marathon. It appeared to have gotten over its terrible twos and was now playing nice.

Today's run was around Rutland Water and I had so many lovely memories associated with this beautiful natural space. It was a favourite place for me to take Riley as he was growing up, we'd done water sports at the centre, we'd cycled it and I'd run stretches of it before. Today I was going to run it all the way around and I had the company of Sharif and Rufus.

So why oh why, having got into a routine of waking up and starting my marathon somewhere between 9am and 10am, did we decide that today we were going to have a lay in, which lead to a late start?

Perhaps it was because it was a Sunday, and we were at home and a lay in sounded like a good plan at the time, unfortunately it didn't have quite the impact that we were hoping for. A lay in bed led to a very slothful morning and by the time we got to Rutland I was feeling well and truly meh.

Routine was going to be key to this adventure and I'd just blown the routine of getting up and getting moving for 9am-ish (the 'ish' covered my faffing time).

I did get going eventually, but I paid for it later in the day when I started to struggle against the wind and the fading light. However, this adventure was all about learning and today's lesson was that I needed to get going as close to 9am as I could so that I didn't lose the plot at the other end of the day.

We had to choose which direction to take around the man-made lake. It was a big loop so we figured that we would run into the wind at some point. However, I think the wind was playing funny buggers with us and it decided to change direction as we moved around the reservoir. We had a head wind for what felt like the entire day.

An upside of starting late, and it's always important to find the upside, was that I was finishing into the early evening, and running at dusk showed a different dynamic to the wildlife around. Dusk brings out little bugs and insects, which brings out birds. We watched and listened to a flight of swallows which were playing on the updrafts, flitting here, swooping there and catching their dinner with the backdrop of a setting sun.

Moments like these were simple, they were magical, and I was so appreciative that I was putting myself in these places of beauty to experience them.

There are a lot of sheep in the fields around Rutland Water and sheep don't seem to worry too much about you running through their fields during the day, but by late afternoon they start getting a bit bolshy.

I know I have an active imagination and that the more tired I get, the more my mind starts thinking weird thoughts, but I was pretty sure that early-evening-bolshy-sheep were a thing. This was not a once-off phenomenon and as my running got slower in the latter weeks of this adventure and the evenings drew in earlier, I noticed this early-evening-bolshy-sheep behaviour again and again.

During the final kilometres of the day, the sheep that we were running past started staring me down and stomping their hooves on the ground as if to say 'What the hell are you doing in my field woman? I entertain you humans all day long. I let you pass through and take photos, but there comes a time in the day when we need to be left in peace, so that we can get on with our own private lives'.

Yep, I believe I now speak fluent sheep.

The tiredness, the lateness of the day and the bitterness of the head wind was perhaps getting to me.

DAY 16. LEICESTER SCHOOLS, LEICESTERSHIRE

Monday 11ᵗʰ September, 2017

Daily distance: 43.0km

Time taken: 5hrs 37mins

Total adventure distance: 683.6km

Being adaptable and changing plans did change the shape of this adventure.

I had originally wanted this to be a running adventure tour of the UK. However, having to stay close to home for stints did bring about other opportunities which I can now say without hesitation gave my adventure more purpose and passion. Today I was heading to Parks Primary School in Leicester for the start of marathon 16.

I'd been to Parks before, way back in 2010 when I was doing my 7in7. On day five I did a running tour of a few of Leicester's inner-city primary schools. My friend, Cas Evans, Head Teacher of Parks Primary School, and her wife Jo, had been instrumental in getting the local primary schools to welcome me and get their students to join me for a little run around their school yard as part of my marathon distance.

Cas, who had been watching my latest adventure via Facebook, noticed that we were currently homebound, and came up with the suggestion of me doing the Leicester school visits again. She sent an email out to all the city schools and the response was phenomenal. Twenty schools responded saying that they would love for me to visit. Jo took the reins again and organised a route that would see me run to ten schools on day sixteen and a further ten schools on day seventeen.

At 9am (this was one of those few days I mentioned, that I was on time), Cas introduced me to her students with a school assembly and the day got underway with an abundance of squealing and cheering as hundreds of little feet joined me running laps around the school grounds. What a noise and what a way to start the day.

Although Cas had some head teacher duties to attend to in the morning, she said she'd join me later in the day, but in the meantime, she'd managed to talk not only some of her own staff, but staff at the schools I'd be visiting, to join me for as much or as little of the run as they could.

The order of primary school visits was Parks, Stokes Wood, Glebelands, Beaumont Lodge, Heatherbrook, Forest Lodge, Braunstone Frith, Christ the King Juniors and Infants, Dovelands, Imperial, Folville, Braunstone Community and Eyres Monsell. That was a lot of kids to chat and run with, what an opportunity. This was going to be a great day.

I was introduced at each school with a school assembly and at each school I asked the students to put their hand up if they liked to run – it was almost always a 100% arm raise.

Then, with a big smile on my face, I asked the children to put both arms up if they **loved** to run. My face lit up as the kids raised both arms and squealed with excitement.

I then went on to ask a series of questions:

'Who could run fast sometimes?' the majority of kids shot their arm into the air. I put my arm in the air, because sometimes I could run fast.

'Who could run slow sometimes?' a few kids put their arm in the air. I raised mine too, explaining that I was sometimes very slow.

'Who ran somewhere in the middle sometimes?' hands were raised and so was mine, and I explained that this was my usual ranking in a race - I was someone who was somewhere in the middle, an average runner.

However, I explained further, sometimes, like now, I was able to take my average and ordinary running skills and achieve something extraordinary.

Whilst I was raising money and awareness for the charity HDA during this adventure, I'd also knew that if these kids took my words on board and realised that you can take a seemingly 'impossible' dream and change it to an *'I'm Possible'* reality, well that was a pretty powerful message and one that I was so grateful to be sharing.

After my short Q&A talk at each of the schools, the students then joined me for a little run around their school grounds.

Kids are great, the fast ones would shoot on by me, yelling out for me to watch how fast they could run and as they looped me, they'd tell me what loop they were on and how great they were.

The kids that ran beside me would also tell me how great they were and how they loved to run and that this was fun.

There were kids who would drop behind me, so I'd slow down hold their hands and tell them how great they were and how strong they looked.

I encouraged them to skip a little, hop like frogs a little, walk a little, and be speedy a little. We laughed and giggled and enjoyed being outside together and I repeated this loop of fun and joy over and over at every school. As the kids ran around their school fields, I took the opportunity for a breather turning in the direction they were coming from and offering my hand up to high five them as they ran past. The high fives came at my hand fast and furious, each kid determined to give me their best. Perhaps, I hadn't thought this part through, but it was worth a slightly sting-ing hand to witness the joy on their faces. Running, squealing, high fiving, having fun - this was lifting me to a whole new level of com-mitment, determination and belief that I could complete this adventure.

As promised, Cas did join me later in the day and as we ran, it began to rain, just a little drizzle. We were on our way to the final school of the day and we knew that we were already racing (and I use the term 'racing' very loosely as at this point I was close to the end of my day and I was sixteen days into the adventure) against the school's closing time so we didn't bother getting our rain jackets out. We ploughed on, sploshing through the puddles until the clouds fully exploded. Taking refuge under a big oak tree, we took stock of the situation. At my pace, we would only just make it to the school and that would give me no time for a talk or a run. As much as I didn't want to, we had to miss the last school and turn back to Cas's school. The Head Teacher of the missed school completely understood, and I promised that I'd make it back at some point during this adventure, but not today.

Back at Parks, I had just a couple of kilometres to go. I shuffled around the streets as Cas headed back inside to dry off and get the ice-creams ready. She knows me well.

As I ran that last little bit, I reflected on the day that I had just experienced. It was so different than my original plans. I'd in-tended to visit 63 different locations throughout the UK for each of my marathons and I expected to run mainly on my own or with small groups of adults for most of the nine weeks. Instead I'd just run around with thousands of kids, I'd shared my story of believing I can, I'd shared my love and joy of running and I had a hope that maybe I had done my little bit in inspiring the next generation.

I also gave thought to the fact that it had taken my body three weeks to adjust to the stresses I was putting it through and driving myself an hour (from Leicester to home) at the end of the day was only now okay. I honestly don't think I would have got to week three if I'd had to do all the running, then the driving as well as the cooking and the getting myself ready, as had been the intention in the original plans.

The adventure was not looking exactly as I had planned, but the experiences I was having, the opportunities I was receiving and the inclusion of Sharif and my friends, and now so many school children, was turning into something far better and more rewarding than I had ever thought.

DAY 17. LEICESTER SCHOOLS, LEICESTERSHIRE

Tuesday 12th September, 2017

Daily distance: 44.1km

Time taken: 5hrs 28mins

Total adventure distance: 727.7km

My second school day was just as exciting, noisy and full of kids telling me how fast they could run as they zoomed past me. It was full of high-fives and a stinging hand, which I didn't mind, and it was full of this thing called dabbing.

I'll try and explain dabbing for those who may be unaware of the dab.

You bring one arm up in front of your face as if you're about to sneeze into your elbow and you lean your head in, whilst your other arm is flung out to the side. Variations of the dab included doing a little jump at the same time, doing a big jump at the same time or doing a lunge that looks like you're about to fly into the person in front of you and head butt them. This seemed to be the most common variation the kids used with me as they came my way.

Having a teenage boy, I'd known what dabbing was all about, but also having a teenage boy I'd been told more than once 'no mum, just no' - apparently dabbing was not a cool thing for a mum to do. Despite knowing this rule, I dabbed back and thankfully these kids, being the non-teenage variety, didn't seem to mind.

Several of the schools I visited wanted to take the participation thing a bit further and had organised small teams of students and teachers to join me for the run to the next school. The day was turning into a marathon relay and I was the baton. The kids were amazing, cruising along keeping to my pace, which was slower than they could run, but they persevered with me as I shuffled along.

By running that little bit further with me and out of the school grounds, I hoped that they were getting that extra sense of how running could be an exciting adventure. It had been for me, and in these smaller groups I was able to share a few more stories of where my feet had taken me.

'Where has been my favourite place to run so far?' was the most commonly asked question throughout the day. My answer that day is the same answer I give now to that question – I genuinely love every run that I get to go on. I may not necessarily enjoy every step of the run, but when I finish and reflect, I'm always so happy and grateful that I can run. That might sound like a bit of a cop-out in that I can't choose my favourite place, but it's true. Running outside is my favourite place to run.

Day seventeen had been another amazing day. Today I managed to reach all ten schools on the route, including Krishna Avanti, Whitehall, Linden, Evington Valley, Avenue, Spinney Hill, Merrydale Juniors, Willowbrook, Northfield House and each school had been filled with amazing noise, cheery chatter and of course, dabbing (don't tell Riley).

DAY 18. GRANTHAM CANAL, NOTTINGHAMSHIRE

Wednesday 13th September, 2017

Daily distance: 42.8km

Time taken: 6hrs 8mins

Total adventure distance: 770.5km

The two days visiting schools had been awesome with so much noise and energy. Today I was back home on my local canal path loops.

It was quiet. Very quiet. It gave me a lot of time to think. Perhaps too much time in that I got a little bit lost in my head rather than in the beauty around me and what I was trying to achieve outside of me.

I ran through the kilometres feeling a little bit lost and a little bit down.

I'd had quite a few emotional days up to this point, I'd also had quite a few uneventful days, but this day was an unusual empty feeling that I hadn't felt before.

I guess the intensity of the previous two days had taken a little bit out of me, but this was a good learning curve. As determined as I was, and as much purpose and passion for the adventure that I had, I still had to get through all the days in those nine weeks, irrelevant of whether I was enjoying every little step or not.

I got through marathon 18 and gave thanks that I was here and that I could (run).

DAY 19. LINCOLN, LINCOLNSHIRE

Thursday 14th September, 2017

Daily distance: 43.0km

Time taken: 5hrs 23mins

Total adventure distance: 813.5km

Day nineteen was the closest I came to not running.

From the thrill and noise of my runs at the start of the week, to the quiet and quite lonely marathon yesterday, my headspace had got into a funk and waking up today my head wasn't playing nice with me.

Today I was heading to Lincoln and I was going to be joined by some locals from the running club Lincolnshire Runners. Sharif had received a text message the night before, letting me know that unfortunately most people had pulled out, but perhaps one person might be able to join me.

In the frame of mind that I was in from the previous day, I questioned what the point was of me driving all the way to Lincoln, which was over an hour's drive from Nottingham, if I was going to run a marathon all by myself.

It wasn't lost on me that this had always been the possible scenario from the original plan. As much as I had wanted people to join me, and the invitation to run with me was out in the world, I knew that occasionally I would be running by myself and that it was up to me to complete all the steps of a marathon day in, day out to get this adventure done. I thought that I had squared that away in my brain.

I think that after the two school visit days where I had felt an even greater depth of purpose to the adventure - the experience of togetherness and teamwork - going back to being on my own again, felt like there was something missing.

I sat at home wondering whether I should continue on with this or not, questioning if I had the right objectives for this run or not, when I received a text message asking where to meet and how far away I was. Well that snapped me out of my malaise, I had a commitment to keep to myself, to the charity, to the people who were taking an interest, to the people that had taken part already and to those who were going to join me at some point in the future. C'mon Nic, move ya butt.

I spent the drive to Lincoln thinking about how I'd nearly thrown it all away. This was not what I'd set out to do. I was not going to give in. I was not going to give up. I arrived in Lincoln back on track mentally and ready for some butt moving.

I realised that I had to come back to terms with the fact that there could be days when I would be alone, but I'd also have days when people would want to join me and be a part of this. I had to stop feeling sorry for myself that this was a small adventure and get on with making it my best adventure.

I arrived in Lincoln a whopping hour and a bit late. Keith Iley, owner of the shop Lincolnshire Runner, and two of the club members, Peter Wells and Ros Treadwell, were patiently waiting for me. I gave them my sincerest apology for I was truly sorry that I'd let my head wander from the objective I'd given it.

Keith explained the route to me, it was a route he'd plotted for another crazy-assed multi-marathon runner, Ben Smith, and that Ben had given it a thumbs up as an easy and quite enjoyable route. Keith asked did I know Ben? I knew of Ben - I had watched him on social media as he ran a whopping 401 marathons in 401 days. Thankfully for me, I was attempting to beat a woman's record on this adventure. I was hoping that I'd get to meet Ben at some point.

Due to my lateness, for which I again apologised profusely, Ros was only able to stay for a lap around our start location, Boultham Park. Peter had a little more time to spare so he was tasked with leading me out of the city and into the countryside, and whilst he couldn't stay for the entire day, he did promise to come back later and run me back through the city and back to Boultham Park to finish my day. I was okay with that plan and I was truly grateful for the company that they'd both provided throughout the morning. Our running conversation mainly centred around the charity that I was running for and this helped me refocus on the purpose of the adventure.

My knowledge of Lincolnshire was that it was a flat, farming county and that Lincoln has a castle and a cathedral which I'd get to see later in the day. The first half was all about seeing the beautiful countryside and I had been informed that I'd be passing one or two ice-cream places along the route, this cheered me up no end. I'll always happily run for ice-cream.

I had been under the impression that the entire county of Lincolnshire was flat, flat as pancake. This wasn't exactly true, there was quite a bit of an incline that I had to run up as I headed from the countryside back into the city.

It did make sense that there was a hill, there was after all a castle in the middle of Lincoln and as was the purpose of castles, to house nobility and to provide its owner with a protective place of vantage to look out over their land, this invariably meant that there was a hill.

Peter had texted me letting me know he was free again and could join me if I wanted the company. Yes please, that would be ace, I replied back. I had settled my head down and I had been enjoying the running alone again, but I'd also decided my tactics for the rest of the adventure would be to accept any company for as little or as long as someone would like to run with me.

Peter caught up with me at the bottom of that 'only' hill in Lincoln. I'd noticed it in the distance and in my head I figured it would be a nice break for me to walk it but Peter wasn't having any of that and he chatted and ran whilst I found the gear to take on the hill. He said that this side of town was the easy incline, wait until I got to the other side, the downhill was a doozy. Well that was something to look forward too.

Another thing I was looking forward to was visiting The Lincolnshire Runner store in the city centre where we were going to make a flying visit and pick me up a brand new pair of shoes as I'd pretty much run this pair into the ground.

I'd visited the store just a week prior to starting this adventure in a beat-up pair of trainers that I had done all my training in. I knew that I needed to get some new trainers and that I'd probably need more than one pair, but that was as far as my research into footwear for running 1650.6 miles had gone.

During that initial visit, I looked nervously at the wall of shoes for sale. The staff looked professional and knowledgeable and I felt a little bit silly asking for trainer advice. I was worried they'd think this was perhaps something I should already have known given that I was a week away from my start date.

I had always followed the normal advice you get about trainers - that you break a new shoe in over time, and that you don't go changing things on or just before your race day, or in my case a week out from the start of this mammoth adventure.

I sheepishly asked for their recommendations. Thankfully there were no 'Are you crazy, woman?!' comments, instead they were really very helpful and recommended the brand Hoka, which I'd never heard of. They got me on the treadmill, testing several models and sizes, videoing my gait in each of them and before I knew it, I was a Hoka convert. It was like putting on a pair of slippers. My feet fell in love with them immediately and they have been my trainer of choice ever since.

My best pal Rosie was also something to look forward to. She was working in Lincoln and had texted me to say that she too was going to join me for the last little bit of the day.

I was so glad to have Rosie and Peter's company. Those dastardly last little bits of the day always hurt physically and mentally. I'd look at my watch, seeing and hearing the beep of the 40km mark, knowing that it meant I only had 2.2kms to go.

On any given day of the week when I wasn't running a marathon per day, I could nip out and knock out 2.2kms quickly without thinking twice or possibly without even changing clothing.

During this adventure, these daily last 2.2kms were driving me nuts. They seemed to last practically as long as the entire rest of the day – which was my drama queen way of thinking. I realised that I was going to have to work on another way to think through these last little bits - a more positive, less drama queen way to embrace this last little distance - but for today I had Peter and Rosie to distract me.

Rosie had brought a box full of chocolate cupcakes, she knows me well. These little chocolate cupcakes were what I focussed on rather than the dastardly last little bits and having a yummy treat waiting for me seemed to work. That end bit still hurt but it was all made better with cake. Mmmmm cake.

DAY 20. GRANTHAM CANAL, NOTTINGHAMSHIRE

Friday 15th September, 2017

Daily distance: 42.4km

Time taken: 7hrs 29mins

Total adventure distance: 855.9km

Another recovery marathon along the canal paths near home. It had only been forty-eight hours since I'd last done this route with my head in such a negative space, however today with a change in attitude, I was genuinely loving it.

I had done so many of my training runs along this path before I started this adventure, and I'd now ran quite a few 'recovery' marathons along here.

Throughout that time, I had watched the wildlife around me. The ducks and swans building their nests, the incubation period of their eggs, the hatching and introduction to the world of their babies and now I was seeing the cygnets and ducklings grow.

Two days ago, I was so lost in my head that I forgot to look up, see out and appreciate the view.

Today I was appreciating being a part of their canal life, or maybe they were a part of mine. I know that today I was feeling connected and I was grateful that I was getting to see this as well as share the story of how I was continuing to make this dream a reality.

I'd been receiving so many lovely comments and messages from people who, although not with me physically, were tuning in each day to see how I was getting on and cheering me along. I would have missed this experience had I thrown it all in and given up after day eighteen.

I ran throughout the day, appreciating what I was seeing and sharing the experiences I was having on social media.

Speaking of social media, I had the pleasure of Katie Holmes for part of my run today. Katie had interviewed me prior to starting this adventure for her blog 'Run Young 50'. During our run together today she mentioned that prior to interviewing me, she'd had a few doubts about whether I could actually run 63 marathons, after all it was a huge undertaking and I didn't have much of a track record. I understood completely, I'd be lying if I said I hadn't had any fleeting doubts prior to me starting, and I had the occasional self-questioning throughout, but I knew that I was always going to give it a go to my best ability.

She mentioned that during the interview she had been swayed by my positive mindset and attitude but after today, she knew I would definitely keep doing my utmost to get to my finish line. Katie offered to take over my Twitter account in an attempt to help get more support and get more people to notice what this 50-year-old woman was doing. I truly appreciated the support and the belief Katie, thank you.

Now this might sound weird at this point in the adventure, for I was always aware that to get to day 63 I would have to run all of the days from the first through to the 62nd, but the enormity of the challenge I had set myself had really only just kicked in.

I had to keep on going and never give up.

DAY 21. SHEFFIELD, SOUTH YORKSHIRE

Saturday 16th September, 2017

Daily distance: 42.8km

Time taken: 6hrs 1mins

Total adventure distance: 898.7km

Stan was fixed, so we were all heading back out on the road.

With the help and support of his workplace, Sharif had arranged to work remotely in the van. It meant that he could travel with me, be in charge of feeding and driving and route planning and contacting people and making coffee and then he'd have a break from me and get to work for his paying employers whilst I ran.

I kept mentioning that he was such a lucky man, and I think I heard him mumble something back. No doubt, it was a similar string of supportive words that he used that first day in John O'Groats when Simon and I had left him on the side of the road to somehow MacGyver the bike back together with only a first aid kit.

We were heading to Sheffield for today's run, my friend Ruth Fox had offered us a place to stay in the evening, which we jumped at. As much as we loved Stan, he wasn't the comfiest place to sleep, so the offer of a bed or couch to sleep on was always graciously accepted. Ruth also mentioned that the Sheffield and Tinsley canal was a very pretty canal that meandered its way from Sheffield to Rotherham. Perfect.

As it was a Saturday, we wanted to start the day with a Parkrun, Ruth recommended the Sheffield Castle Parkrun, as it was close to her home. Hmmm, Sheffield Castle? Well that sounded a bit hilly. However, as Sharif pointed out, I was going to spend most of the day down low on a canal, so for the first 5kms I could suck it up and run on some hills.

We'd got into quite a good routine, where I'd moan and Sharif would listen, ignore me, and then kick me out the door espousing his love for me – tough love.

I'm not the most punctual person in the world, it's something I say I'd like to work on, but I know if it was a thing that I'd truly like to change, I would. Instead, I dither about sometimes making things on time and sometimes not. Today was a not.

We arrived at the start of the Sheffield Castle Parkrun approximately ten minutes late, it was probably more like 12 minutes, but hey what was a few more minutes between friends. As well as running a marathon, I now had an extra mini goal within the bigger goal and that was to chase down the tail-walker and make up those ten or so minutes over the 5km course.

Sharif was an avid Parkrun runner before we met, and he was keen to add Sheffield Castle Park to his 'Parkrun tourist' list. During one of our early conversations, he'd shared his list of running rules with me, one of them being to never finish last in a Parkrun or any race for that matter. At the time we'd both figured that this should have been an easy rule to comply with. Today we were going to be testing it.

As I suspected, it was quite an up and down course, but it was a stunning course, the elevation of the park provided a beautiful vantage point to take in the city of Sheffield and because of the hills we were able to see the tail-walker just ahead as we neared the finish line. We were gaining ground; we were having a little game of cat and mouse.

Sharif was by my side urging me on, 'C'mon Nic, we can take them. We can. Keep pushing. Keep pushing ... You what?'

My tummy was grumbling big time, and I desperately needed to go to the loo.

Instead of urging me to chase down the tail walker, Sharif was now urging me to hold on until the end. I was so close and there was a toilet and there were people around and ...

I was trying, I truly was, I knew I only had a few hundred metres to go but nope, I had to go now. I ducked into some heavy bushes and jungle pooed.

The organisers knew that I was on the course, and that I'd been behind the tail-walker, so when the tail-walker crossed the finish line, they decided to send someone out to check on me.

Sharif was now on jungle poo look out patrol and was passing back the vital information that I needed as I was trying to sort out my tummy problems - 'People are coming, pull your shorts up woman.'

I ducked back out of the bushes, just as the search party arrived, then together we ran to the finish line accepting a great big cheer from the kind folk who had waited patiently to see me finish. As for that rule about not coming last in a ParkRun, well Sharif very gallantly broke his rule and let me finish ahead of him. He really is the best, isn't he?

Barring the dodgy belly, this was a lovely start to my day. I now only had another 37.2kms to go and thankfully most of it was going to be along the canal.

We hadn't done much research into today's route, so to make sure that I had enough food and water for the rest of the day Sharif switched from running to cycling, to keep me company along the Sheffield and Tinsley canal and to carry all the stuff.

My tummy movements had been following a pattern. The first 5kms of my day usually involved a bit of rumbling and squeamishness until I relieved myself and then it settled down for the rest of the day.

Today, it had decided to follow a different pattern of not settling at all. I ran along the canal with pretty much one thought in mind 'where's the next toilet?'.

The canal through Sheffield was indeed very pretty, but the city scape soon became industrial estates and the canal path too became quite rough, rugged, overgrown and unkempt, which ultimately did work to my benefit. The further out of town I ran, the fewer people I saw and the more opportunity I had to dash into urban jungles and well, umm, you can figure that out for yourself.

To keep my mind off my dodgy belly, today's topic of conversation was favourite movies. As I ran and Sharif pedalled, we shared our list of favourite movies, both putting forward cases for the movies to determine which order we were going to watch said movies when I wasn't running a stooopid adventure – a more normal time.

Having said that, 'a more normal time' was also a topic we talked quite a bit about. Not much about our first six months together had been 'normal'. We didn't have a TV back at our home as we'd opted to listen to music in the evenings, as such, sitting down and watching TV or movies was not our usual habit – we were actually craving a more unnormal time for us.

As we ran along the canal, we passed a lake full of swans, and you'll probably never guess in a million years what the name of the lake was … yep, Swan Lake (in case you were scratching your head).

It set me off on a little story, and possibly a bit of a rant, to Sharif.

When I was a little girl, I had big dreams of becoming a ballerina. I wanted to dance the lead in the ballet, Swan Lake. I trained from the age of 4, throwing everything I had into ballet.

At the age of 14, I auditioned to attend the feeder school for the Australian Ballet Company and was told I should lose weight, my legs were too big, I was not good enough. I was devastated, but I was determined. I committed myself to more lessons, more hours of practice – all good to improve my technique.

Unfortunately, I dealt with the information about my body shape and weight not quite so good. It started a period of bulimic tendencies. Wanting to lose weight and change the shape of my thighs I changed my eating habits which mainly consisted of me eating hardly anything of substance and consuming more boxes of chocolate laxatives than a 14 year old should have been able to buy. Making myself throw up was a regular occurrence, as well as training with sweatpants on (sweatpants are plastic pants that I'd slip over the top of my ballet tights and leotard). I slept in sweatpants too with my electric blanket turned up to high throughout the night. Not surprising I lost weight but the following year I still didn't make the cut and gave up on the thing that I had absolutely loved – ballet.

It was a few years later, in an aerobics class at my local gym that the head instructor, Elaine, took me aside after a class. She told me how good I was at her classes, how strong and bouncy I was, how my athleticism, my musicality, my legs – yes, my legs – were perfect for aerobics. She suggested that maybe I should become an instructor.

At age 19, I went to night school and became an aerobics/gym instructor, and from that point on my job became to encourage, inspire and help people look after, love and care for their body and their minds, and I've been doing it ever since.

Running 63 marathons in 63 days was yet another way to be the instructor and show 'how' and 'what' you can achieve when you put your mind to it. I was so grateful for Elaine's comments all those years ago, I'd created such a bad association with my legs, turns out they are pretty awesome at the whole runny, bouncy, jumpy stuff.

As I stood on the edge of Swan Lake, all the swans, and there were a whole lotta swans, headed my way. I assume they thought I'd give them some food. Sorry swans, these legs needed all the food I was carrying to get me through my day. With all the swans gathered in front of me, I mentioned that it looked like a corps de ballet and I took my opportunity whilst I had it. I danced a few of the steps I could remember from the ballet Swan Lake. I'd eventually made it – I'd become the lead!

Sharif took a happy snap for me to able to reminisce in my much older years – that time I danced the lead of Swan Lake! Happy days.

Ruth was waiting back at the start of the Sheffield and Tinsley Canal Trail in the city centre. She had some good news to urge me on, there was an ice-cream shop open and waiting for me. Ah, the little things that can get me going.

I was still a few hundred metres short of the full marathon distance as we entered the quay, so tantalisingly close to the ice-cream parlour but I couldn't stop yet. I pushed on, choosing the flavour I'd eventually have as I shuffled past the shop window. I also shuffled past tables of people who were settling into Saturday afternoon relax mode. This hit me with a bit of a whammy, seeing so many people sitting together, enjoying the afternoon with a glass of wine or a pint of beer, just watching the day go by. I missed my weekends of being able to pop to the pub, not having exhausted myself throughout the day, and then not having to worry about getting up the next day to exhaust myself running again the following day.

Sharif quickly brought my mind back to what I was doing and why. There'd be plenty of time at the end of this adventure to do all the stuff that we'd talked about – the unnormal stuff.

Finally finishing outside the ice-cream parlour, I saw that the shop had my most favourite ice-cream, lemon sorbet – winning! With my ice-cream in hand, we wandered off to Ruth's car, which she informed us was a bit of walk away. Never mind, I had ice-cream to ease my weary body. Ruth also told us that she had a home-made stew on the stove that would be ready for when we got in, but to placate my weary body even more we'd head home via her local pub. Ruth knew we liked to have a pint at the end of the day and have a pint at the end of the day we were going to do.

An ice-cream, a pint, a home-made stew and a couch to pass out on, I was one very happy gal.

I didn't really mean to pass out on the couch, Ruth did have a spare room for us, but I mentioned that I'd just have a little laydown over there on the couch so that I could still listen in on the conversation everyone was having around the dinner table and that was me, I was gone for the night.

From your birth to end
Learn, reflect, design your path
Love where your life leads

~ Nikki Love

WEEK 4

DAY 22. HUDDERSFIELD, WEST YORKSHIRE

Sunday 17th September, 2017

Daily distance: 42.8km

Time taken: 6hrs 7mins

Total adventure distance: 941.5km

The Huddersfield Narrow Canal was the venue for the start of week four's marathons.

As I mentioned, I'd fallen in love with the UK's canal system as running along a canal tended to mean that the location was relatively flat, that is unless there are a lot of locks. There are a lot of locks along the Huddersfield Narrow Canal.

The upside of running an out and back along a canal with a lot of locks is that one of the directions would be downhill and I'd chosen well, the 'out' was uphill, therefore meaning the 'back' was downhill, woohoo!

Marsden is located just north of the Peak District National Park, which is renowned for its rugged hills and wilderness, but that didn't mean the scenery stopped at the edge of the National Park.

The canal between Marsden and Huddersfield carved its way through rugged hills and lush countryside in which every shade of green and brown had been displayed. The path took me through some quiet woodlands, past historic mills and through quaint little villages, all the while the sounds of the water in the narrow canal soothed my mind.

I really do love running in places like this. I get lost in the scenery and the sounds – it's quiet and yet there is always noise. Maybe it's my brain that goes quiet?

Sharif rode beside me again today, but there was less chatter and more simply taking in the beauty of where we were. Today running was easy.

We had intended to run in an outward direction until I reached the half marathon distance then turn back, but this little thing called the Standedge Tunnel, which is the longest, deepest and highest canal tunnel in the country, got in the way. It takes a canal boat three hours to get through the tunnel and it's not open to people on foot.

Above the tunnel there was a whopping big mountain of a hill, which apparently did have a walk path that went up and over that we could have taken to get to the other end of the tunnel. But looking at the whopping big mountain of a hill, we opted to do a turnabout and make up the distance by running past our start location and doing a loop back to the finish.

It meant that I would be finishing going back 'up', but it would only be for a mile or so. 'You can do that can't you?', Sharif asked. I responded with a yes, so long as he agreed to buy me a slice of chocolate cake and ice-cream at the shop that we had intended to stop at but would now be running past. I explained that I very much doubted that I would make it through those last few miles without that cake and ice-cream safely in my belly.

He agreed wholeheartedly, he'd been dreaming about the cake too, and sure enough I was able to finish those final miles back up the hill.

DAY 23. ROCHDALE CANAL, LANCASHIRE

Monday 18th September, 2017

Daily distance: 42.8km

Time taken: 6hrs 17mins

Total adventure distance: 984.3km

Rochdale was one of the original 63 locations that I had really wanted to make it to. Rochdale was where I was born.

I'd been to Rochdale a few times in my adult life, but I didn't know it all that well. I knew that my parents had lived there as newly-weds and that although they had a circle of close friends, they never really considered it home and were keen to get away. They considered the US for a time, but eventually opted for Australia and left for the land down under when I was a little over a year old.

Their two closest Lancastrian friends, John and Wendy Cullen, were my Godparents. Wendy still lived in Rochdale, but John had passed away when he was only 51 years of age. Today's start location was at the church where John had been buried.

Whilst starting at the church felt good, it did lead to some interesting thoughts throughout the day. John's life had ended at 51, and here I was at 50 and a half, only now fully realising what it was that I wanted to do with my life.

That probably sounds far more over-dramatic than it needed to be. I was happy with my life. I had been doing things that I enjoyed and that I loved, and I had given birth and raised a wonderful son.

It's just that I had secretly wanted to be this person who ran adventures, who wrote and told stories about them and who encouraged and inspired others to go after their own goals and dreams.

Up until taking on this adventure I had been afraid of fully admitting and committing myself to achieving this goal. Committing to becoming that person meant that I would have to see this adventure through all the way to its completion – after all, a writer and speaker of running adventures had to have some epic running adventures to write and speak about.

I'd also then have to write and speak about the adventure. I know this probably sounds a bit weird, as I was quite happy taking selfies and videos of me running here, running there, working out in my garden, at the beach, in the park, wherever I happened to be, but I was not always keen on sharing stories of emotions and previous experiences that had shaped me. And these were going to be relevant in keeping me going every single day of this adventure. I'd have to share the good, the bad and the ugly, as they were all there in real life.

The reason I was here now, doing what I was doing, was that I had read the books written by amazing and inspiring people such as Rosie Swale Pope MBE and Dean Karnazes and I'd been totally wowed by their amazingness. Their words had lit a little fire in my own belly and a thought of wonderment in my mind 'Could I do something like that? I wonder what I'm capable of achieving.'

I had been encouraging, inspiring and helping people since the age of 19. I'd been working in the fitness industry as an aerobics instructor, gym instructor, personal trainer, run coach, bootcamp coach, sports massage therapist for over thirty years. I now wanted to encourage, inspire and help people in this new medium. I wanted to be the person who helped someone like me who was reading about the running adventures of a fifty-and-a-half-year-old woman and thinking that maybe they could do this too.

I knew deep down that this had been one of my WHYs, it was just one that I really hadn't fully admitted until today. I ran through Rochdale, where my life started, and let these thoughts settle in.

My whole life started here and all the things that came after my birth had shaped me to be the person I am today. The choices that my parents had made in moving halfway around the world to Australia and raising me in a country that was sport oriented and was big on girls being involved as well as boys. I know I benefited from the Aussie culture of being outdoors, being sporty and growing up in a country that invested in an extremely wide variety of grass roots sports.

I ran along the Rochdale canal trying to wonder what life would have been like if my parents had decided to stay. Different was the best answer I could come up with.

The UK canal system was benefitting from the upsurge in bike riding and the influx of money from the Government to create cycling paths, which were often incorporated into already established canal paths. It made sense, the canal paths got upgraded, it took bikes away from very busy and polluted roads and the canal paths on the whole were wide enough for us all to use ... or so I thought.

Today I ran into, well it was more like he ran into me, a cyclist who had decided that the whole of the path was there for him and was not to be shared. He brushed past me, yep that close, so I yelled my consternation at his riding capabilities. He stopped and yelled back that maybe I should get out of his way.

I was keen to point out that it was in fact he who had come up behind me, and that he didn't ring a bell or shout out for me to move over, and that it was he who'd brushed by me ... but really I couldn't be bothered.

Instead I stopped, grabbed some food and water and waited patiently until he rode off.

Up until that point I'd had a lovely time running along the Rochdale canal, chatting to walkers, saying hi to other riders, running alongside the deepest canal in the UK, and I was not going to let him ruin my running buzz.

I only really had this one bad experience with a cyclist, on the whole I found cyclists to be happy and friendly co-users of the canal paths and this really was a very pretty and pleasant way to move through the countryside and in between major cities, for everyone.

DAY 24. LEEDS, WEST YORKSHIRE

Tuesday 19th September, 2017

Daily distance: 42.6km

Time taken: 5hrs 52mins

Total adventure distance: 1026.9km

We spent the night in Leeds with friends Kris King and Clare Gill. Kris greeted me at his door with the comment 'Why do you always look so beaten up when I see you?'.

Kris is the owner of the Beyond the Ultimate race series, of which the JungleUltra is a race. And for five days I'd run in extreme humidity, jungle undergrowth, deep mud. I'd completed more than 50 river crossings, and often found myself running into the darkness – I'm not a big fan of running at night when I'm at home, running at night in a jungle is simply terrifying. I was covered from head to toe in mud, bruises, scrapes, rashes, blisters, so yes, I looked pretty beaten up throughout those five days.

Although I was no longer in a jungle, and I didn't have any scrapes, bruises or blisters (in fact my feet hadn't had one blister up to this point), it seemed that I still looked pretty knocked about.

I looked rough because of my tummy issues. I was struggling to get enough food in. As fast as I was eating it, I seemed to be losing it out the other end. Now I know that's not quite the way the digestive system works, there is a processing time, but it felt like it was an immediate reaction.

It was an issue I knew I needed to address, however, tonight's issue that I had to discuss with Kris was that I had foolishly booked myself into another of his races, the DesertUltra, before I had worked out the dates for my 63 marathons adventure.

The DesertUltra, much like the JungleUltra, is an extreme race in extreme conditions. This one is a 250km, five-day self-supported run through the oldest desert in the world, the Namib Desert, in temperatures that often soared above 50 degrees Celsius.

If everything continued going to my current plan, I'd be finishing my 63 marathons on the 28th October, just a couple of weeks before I was supposed to head to Namibia and run through a desert.

Kris took one look at me and agreed, I wasn't going to make it this year. Sure, the mileage would be in my legs, but this adventure was draining me, and it was dangerous in the desert. Much like the jungle, there were real live animals and conditions that could kill me. I had to be in tip top form to take on a challenge like that. That little adventure was going to have to wait a year.

(A little side note, I did eventually make it to Namibia for the 2019 DesertUltra event and sure enough, it was a stooopidly insane adventure race and I nearly died – which may be a little bit drama queenish – I did get lost and was absolutely terrified but that's another story for another book).

That took a bit of a load off my mind, all I had to think about was getting through day 24. I did my best to eat the chicken and potatoes that Kris and Clare had prepared, but mainly I nibbled and then passed out.

Before taking off in the morning, we had a chat about Huntington's Disease. Kris's family had been impacted by the disease and he too had done some extraordinary challenges to raise money and awareness for research into the eradication of the gene. Even though I was tired, I was having belly troubles and I looked rough, I still had a fire in my belly to get on with this adventure and to do as much as I could for the charity. Our morning chat spurred me on for the day.

The Leeds canal was beckoning, and I had a rendezvous with another HDA campaigner, Jackie Harrison. Jackie's family had been ripped apart by the disease, and although I knew her story would be heart-breaking, I also believed, as did she, that it would also be a story of tenacity, determination, hope and an abundance of love, and in sharing it, we could raise more money and awareness for such a worthy cause.

Riding alongside me, Jackie started by saying how happy she was to be outside on such a lovely day but couldn't stay all day as she was the primary carer for her brother, Mark. She showed me pictures of Mark and then shared the story of her family as we moved along the canal.

Huntington's had been passed along through generations of her family and they'd lost her grandfather, her uncle and her mother to the disease. Both Jackie and Mark were still young when their 48-year-old mum lost her battle with the disease. Their dad had left their family unit unable to cope with the stresses and it was Jackie's grandmother, who by this stage had lost her husband and both her son and daughter to the disease, who looked after them. She too passed away, and at the age of 18, Jackie sought legal guardianship for her 12-year-old brother and became both sister and responsible adult for Mark. Devastatingly, Mark too was diagnosed with Huntington's and as the disease progressed and Mark's motor-skills degenerated, Jacqui also became Mark's fulltime health carer. *

It was a harrowing story, but Jackie was keen to point how smart and driven Mark had been and how he'd completed a degree in English from the University of Leeds, he'd read all of Shakespeare's plays and had a degree in history from the University of Huddersfield, unfortunately he'd been unable to start his career as the disease gripped his body.

Jackie was also keen to tell me about the fun and happy times she was still able to share with Mark and how they now used social media to bring the outside world back into his life. They held a weekly singing corner using Facebook Live, singing all of Mark's favourites tunes. Jackie said they'd sing something for me during their next sing-along – I was very honoured.

Just before Jackie said goodbye to me for the day, she handed me a toy 'Sybil' dog to take with me on my journeys. Jackie had been hand-making little stuffed dogs based on their border terrier 'Sybil' and had created a community 'Hounds4Huntingtons' to raise awareness of the disease world-wide. I accepted my little Sybil and promised that it was now part of my team and would go everywhere with me. Sybil still travels with me in my backpack and pops up every now and again in my social media stories.

Whilst I was running along the canal with Jackie, Sharif had been testing out his 'drive ahead and remotely work in the van' tactic. It was working nicely which was another weight off both our shoulders – he could maintain his work commitment and keep paying our bills and I could do the easy bit and keep running like a runny thing.

As he was in the van, and the Leeds canal stretched for 127 miles, rather than do an out and back I kept running along taking in the beauty of the area, checking out the quaint and sometimes eccentric narrow boats and enjoying several ice-creams along the way.

As I ran with an ice-cream hanging out of my mouth, I received a comment from a chap sitting by the canal watching the day roll by 'Should you be running and eating an ice-cream?' Yes, my friend, absolutely yes!

With great sadness, I have to share that Mark Harrison passed away on 7th September, 2019 at 47 years young. RIP Mark.

DAY 25. LADY BOWER RESERVOIR, DERBYSHIRE

Wednesday 20th September, 2017

Daily distance: 42.6km

Time taken: 6hrs 31mins

Total adventure distance: 1069.5km

Lady Bower Reservoir had been another location from my original list.

There was an annual trail marathon held in the area and the pictures of the location were amazing. I had been there once before during a holiday visit to the UK, many years prior to me eventually moving to the UK. I'd driven along the road, Snake Pass, which winds its way through the Peak District and around the reservoir – I remembered the views from that drive, and I was very much looking forward to running around the area.

Sharif joined me for my first half hour, he then doubled back to the van to start his day of work whilst I continued running along the banks of the reservoir.

I'd been noticing the slight changes in the season as I ran along the canals, but out here amongst the sweeping hills of the Derwent Valley, I was able to see the full impact of autumn. Pockets of the most brilliant reds, yellows and oranges were bursting out amongst the lush greens of the heavily wooded hills.

It had been a while since I'd run in such a remote place. Along the canals I'd run through quiet countryside, but I'd also passed through small villages in between the major towns. Once Sharif left me today, I ran past the occasional dog walker as well as one or two anglers who were blissfully enjoying the quietness of the area before being rudely interrupted by the huffing and puffing of a crazy woman, and that was about it.

With a few kilometres to go, I came off the trail and back onto the road where Sharif and Stan the Van were parked up, mainly to let Sharif know I was still alive and running, but also for my own peace of mind that people were still around and about - I'd spent hours on my own out on these trails. To my surprise my friend from Sheffield, Ruth, had turned up with a Tupperware container full of home-cooked stew, she was concerned about my belly and me looking so tired and rough.

Grabbing some cuddles and some words of encouragement from both Ruth and Sharif, I surged on along the road, keen to get this marathon finished and get some stew into my belly.

Running back to the van, I received some cheers and high fives from complete strangers that I passed and wondered how they knew. There was also a little crowd waiting at the van for me, Ruth had been busy whilst I was finishing my last little bit telling everyone and anyone that she saw what I was doing and asked them to give me a little cheer.

It was a lovely and loud way to finish what was a very quiet and lonely, but spectacularly scenic marathon.

DAY 26. GRANTHAM CANAL, NOTTINGHAMSHIRE

Thursday 21st September, 2017

Daily distance: 42.7km

Time taken: 7hrs 14mins

Total adventure distance: 1112.2km

We'd headed back home after yesterday's marathon – Sharif needed to actually 'go' to work and I was happy to be running another recovery marathon after five days of being on the road and dealing with a dodgy belly.

The mundane recovery marathon was much needed. I was able to carry less in my backpack, but I ate more as I popped home after each of my canal loops.

I scootched up and down the canal doing a 12km loop three times, a 5km loop once and a few mini loops around my house to finish, and when Sharif returned home I happily reported back to him about my day:

Canal life was just as I'd left it, but the cygnets and ducklings were growing. My canal friend, Canal Peter, had been out walking his dog Diesel every day – we'd chatted, and he'd told me he thought I was nuts. It had rained, I'd got soaked but it had been a good marathon day.

Running a marathon every day was feeling quite *Groundhog Day*'ish. It was same/same, but each one just a little different and each one bringing me closer to achieving my goal and making this dream a reality.

DAY 27. WATERMEAD & RIVER SOAR, LEICESTERSHIRE

Friday 22nd September, 2017

Daily distance: 42.7km

Time taken: 5hrs 57mins

Total adventure distance: 1154.9km

Although back at home, I fancied a slight change of scenery, somewhere flat and that I knew like the back of my hand.

I'd lived in Leicester for a period of ten years and throughout the years I'd lead bootcamps around the lakes of Watermead Country Park and running clubs along the paths of the Soar River. My old fitness haunts were today's playground.

Arriving at Watermead Country Park, I had one of those flashback moments. During my 7in7 adventure I had run number six here at Watermead. I had a big crowd of people join me that day. I had formed some wonderful friendships with the mums of Riley's school mates, and as well as look after me during the week, running some bits with me, giving me lifts, and ensuring that I had food to eat in the evenings (I genuinely hadn't thought that part of the logistics through and without their help cooking food for me, I'm not sure what I would have done), my girlfriends had all turned up that 7in7 morning with their own kids to loop around the country park with me.

Whilst there was lots of noise and support and giggles and fun (the kids were having a ball), there was a lot of crying too – mostly from me. Well actually, all the crying was from me, I was in so much pain running that marathon. Everything hurt and I kept running whilst everything hurt. I know I repeated myself then, but I was in so much pain that day.

Today I was tired, but that was it, my legs were absorbing each and every 42.2kms that I lay before them. I was grateful that my body was adapting to the task I'd set it and that my mind was strong and focussed. I was thankful that I'd not given up on my dream to try this multi-day, multi-week, multi-month adventure once more.

It had taken me seven years to be brave enough to take the action, with most people telling me to forget about it – didn't I remember just how bad I felt way back in 2010?

Yes, I remembered the pain vividly, but instead of wanting to forget about it and say well that was as good as I was ever going to get, I wanted to go back to it, and be the big-dreamer who went after her audacious goals. I wanted to make changes, implement the things I had learned the hard and painful way from that first experience, and I wanted to see if I could improve.

That's what personal growth is all about, it's what I coached, trained and mentored people about. It's not easy the first time, you make mistakes, it hurts, you learn, but if you keep persevering, implement new tactics from learned mistakes, and believe that you can improve with determination, perseverance and resilience then you will find that you are capable of more than you thought possible.

I left the country park and ran along the River Soar; these were the paths that I had coached and trained and urged so many women to believe that they could run. I ran with a little tear in my eye, not from pain this time around, but from pride that I had never given up.

If you are reading this with a great big goal dream inside your head that you think sounds crazy, and everyone around you thinks is crazy too, and you've started second guessing and letting fears and doubts creep in, and the voices of the naysayers are getting louder and louder. I urge you to stop and re-read the title of my book. I ran 63 marathons in 63 days. It was not easy, it took a lot of hard work but I took the word impossible and made it *'I'm Possible'*, so whatever you have in your mind – I believe you can do it too.

DAY 28. COLWICK PARK, NOTTINGHAMSHIRE

Saturday 23rd September, 2017

Daily distance: 42.9km

Time taken: 6hrs 9mins

Total adventure distance: 1197.8km

Another Saturday provided another opportunity to incorporate another Parkrun into my day, and being at home, meant it would be my 'home' Parkrun.

Colwick Park was one of my 'loops from home' runs, and I had intended to run to the start, but the Parkrun starts at 9am which would have required me getting up and running way before my 9am goal start time and that goal start time was still a stretch for me on the best of days and guess what ... yeah, it didn't happen. My lazy butt did not want to get up any earlier than it needed to.

Instead, Sharif made the smart decision of driving us to Colwick Park for the Parkrun. It meant we were able to take Rufus along (Sharif ran with her on the lead), and I was able to have a little chat, whilst not running, with some local friends at the start line.

It also meant that I had 'fresh' legs, well fresh for the day, and I was able to keep a solid pace up that made sure I wasn't last. Sharif was very grateful, as he was not so keen to be as gentlemanly as he'd been the week prior and come last on my behalf at his 'home' Parkrun.

Parkrun completed; I now had a little errand to run - today I was trotting off to collect my race number for the Nottingham marathon being held tomorrow. My long out and back along the River

Trent took me straight past the start/finish line of the Nottingham Marathon.

The marathon carnival was in full swing – the registration tents were being erected and people, local and from all around the world, were filing in to collect their numbers, t-shirts and other marathon paraphernalia. I spoke to a couple of Germans who had flown in to give this marathon a go. I loved the fact that marathon running was not only an event, but it was also an 'experience' that enticed people to travel far and wide to immerse themselves in.

There was an air of excitement at the marathon village as people wandered and jogged about the start line. I too was excited, I was finally coming face to face with an old nemesis and I was feeling strong, feisty and ready … all I had to do was just get today's marathon out of the way first.

If at first, you don't
Your story can t.b.c.
'Til your happy end

~ Nikki Love

WEEK 5

DAY 29. NOTTINGHAM MARATHON, NOTTINGHAMSHIRE

Sunday 24th September, 2017

Daily distance: 43.5km

Time taken: 6hrs 39mins

Total adventure distance: 1241.3km

I'd gratefully accepted an entry into the Nottingham marathon as it was my home-town marathon, which was a nice twist, but it was also that very first marathon that I had DNF'd and I had a bit of unfinished business that I wanted to attend to.

Being my home-town, I knew a lot of people who were also going to be running the course, including Sharif who'd sweetly advised that he was not going to run it alongside me as he was setting out to 'race' it, not shuffle it – cheeky sod.

I didn't mind, because as well as the other 12,000 people who were going to be crossing the start line with me, I had the guaranteed company of Dirk for the first half and Arwen for the entire distance.

We only live a few kilometres away from the start line, so it made perfect sense to walk to the venue to loosen me up and prepare me for what I knew was going to be a pretty emotional day. This obviously meant that I had to get up extra early, but I conceded it was special enough for me to forego those extra few minutes in bed.

Dirk had decided that he was going to run the first half of the marathon with Arwen and me. Now I may not have mentioned it before, but Dirk and Arwen had once been married and they have a son, Henry. We were there not only to raise money for the charity Huntington's Disease Association, but to raise awareness that this is horrible disease, it is extremely difficult to live with, it is hereditary with each descendant having a 50/50 chance of carrying the gene, and that at this point in time there is still no cure.

These are all tough realities of the disease, but things that neither Dirk nor Arwen like to dwell upon. Instead, they concentrate on the here and now and living their best lives. It was from that space of thought and purpose, that we were setting out today - to have a fun day out on the streets of Nottingham, albeit tough fun, because a marathon, even for a great cause, is still a bloody long way.

The sun was shining, the party music was blaring, the gun went off and Dirk, Arwen, me and the 12,000 other excited runners jiggled and rundanced our way along the starting coral until we officially crossed the starting line and our day was underway.

Arwen and I tried to stay on either side of Dirk as he zig-zagged his way along the path. Huntington's Disease is slowly destroying Dirk's brain and it impacts his motor skills, his balance, his memory, his moods and put simply, every aspect of his life. Trying to keep a 'racing line' with Dirk was near impossible.

The Nottingham marathon is a figure 8 course in which all the runners complete the first 13 mile loop together, eventually converging back to the start/finish where those finishing the half marathon finish and those going on for the full, go on.

The plan had been for Dirk to complete the half and Arwen and me to continue on. However, as we got nearer the halfway point Dirk said he wanted to go on. He was feeling good and he didn't know if he'd ever get the opportunity again to run a marathon, and as much as I wanted to say 'you never know', the chances were that this indeed would be the last time that he'd be able to run a full marathon without aid.

As we ran, both Arwen and I started contacting the necessary people about Dirk's decision, we were going to need back up in case Dirk wasn't able to make it all the way. Dirk's wife Jane was waiting at the half-way finish line, she needed to know that we were going to be a few more hours yet. Dirk's mates offered to assist and be ready to pick him up if he was unable to keep going.

Oky doky then, we were going to make this happen.

The distance did start taking its toll on Dirk, he zig-zagged more, he stumbled more, he fell over, he got back up again, but all the while still smiling and laughing. Our mutual friend, Jonny, had taken it upon himself to be our motivational coach, riding alongside us shouting phrases such as 'c'mon you worms' and 'c'mon you slugs' as we shuffled along. Blokes and their banter.

Dirk's pace was slowing and both he and Arwen suggested that I run on as the pace was impacting my running and I had more than just this marathon to think about. I left them in the capable hands of Jonny the master motivator and upped my speed from slug to turtle.

Sharif had indeed raced the day finishing way ahead of me, but rather than rest his weary legs, in true support crew style he got on board Scotty the Bike and found me shortly after I left Dirk and Arwen.

Sharif cycled alongside me until I reached the start of the final two hundred metres – those dastardly final little bits.

Railings had been installed to create a finish avenue for the runners to run along and for the crowds to stand behind and cheer the runners through. The crowds had long gone, except for a small but raucous group waiting patiently. I gratefully accepted the cheers and whistles from Dirk's family and friends, Arwen's family and friends and my own family cheer squad of Riley and Sharif.

Today's dastardly final little bits had been a little less dastardly, I even managed a bit of a sprint finish ... well maybe I moved from turtle pace to, let's say, a baby hare.

I joined the raucous rabble and before too long we heard Dirk whooping and cheering as he, Arwen and Henry, who'd jumped the fence to join his parents, made their way down the home stretch. Dirk's determination and persistence, as well as his naked torso – he'd removed his top earlier in the day due to suffering extreme nipple chaffing – was on show for all to see. I'm not exactly sure where he'd managed to pick up a cigarette in the final couple of hundred metres, but as he charged towards the finish line puffing away, the commentator mentioned that it was not the most conventional of finishes.

Celebration time, and the raucous rabble now at full contingency with Dirk and Arwen headed to the pub to give cheers to Arwen's stamina at keeping Dirk going, to Phil (Arwen's husband) who had aced his race, to Sharif who'd not quite got the time he had wanted but was happy none-the-less, to Jonny and his motivational quips, and to Dirk for his 'farewell to marathon running' marathon.

As for me, I'd run my 29th marathon in a row and I had well and truly dealt with my 2001 Nottingham Marathon DNF. I had created the bedtime story for my boy that I was proud to tell.

DAY 30. GRANTHAM CANAL, NOTTINGHAMSHIRE

Monday 25th September, 2017

Daily distance: 42.7km

Time taken: 6hrs 21mins

Total adventure distance: 1284km

Whilst most of the 12,000 who had run the Nottingham half and full marathon the day before had today as their rest day, I got up and ran my recovery marathon route as my recovery.

Five weeks into this adventure and the routine of running a marathon a day had become a habit.

DAY 31. NOMAD WAY, DERBYSHIRE

Tuesday 26th September, 2017

Daily distance: 43.5km

Time taken: 6hrs 19mins

Total adventure distance: 1327.5km

I forgot to mention that Neil Byford, from marathon 13, had also run Sunday's Nottingham marathon.

Not only did he ace his race, he then made his way to where Arwen, Dirk and I were shuffling through Colwick Park, which was approximately the 19 mile mark, joined us for an extra couple of miles to let me know that he was available this coming Tuesday to run another marathon with me, he then called it a day and headed home. Neil is a running machine.

I'd listed the Nomad Way around Derby as a marathon route in my original plans, and knowing the route well, as it was the paths that he did most of his training along, Neil had offered to lead the way for me today.

The sun was shining as we cruised along the bank of the River Trent having conversations with the folks who were travelling along on their canal boats. We chatted together, we stayed quiet for stretches, I was enjoying this way of life ... put your trainers on and run.

Along the route we spoke more about his dad who has Huntington's Disease, and how this adventure was encouraging Neil to think about his own running ambitions. He was keen to push his own physical boundaries and think a little more outside of the box (which was definitely where my imagination lived) to see what he was capable of achieving as well as help others.

Since helping me with my marathons, Neil is now racing ultras. I say 'racing', as he is such a good runner, that his times often put him at the top end of the leader board of the races he partakes in. He has also become a guide-runner for visually impaired athletes, which combines his qualities of running ability and true kindness and empathy for others.

DAY 32. WATERMEAD & ABBEY PARK, LEICESTERSHIRE

Wednesday 27th September, 2017

Daily distance: 43.2km

Time taken: 6hrs 9mins

Total adventure distance: 1370.7km

Today was literally the day of the football analogy 'a game of two halves'.

The first half of today's marathon was signalling the end of the first half of this whole adventure, the point at which I'd reached that pinnacle and from then on I only had thirty-one and a half more marathons to run, it was all downhill from there ... figuratively speaking.

For the morning session I was joined by two of my massage clients and friends, Katherine Lang and Geeta Patni. Both ladies greeted me with big cuddles and then their concerns that they'd be a bit slow. They genuinely had little to worry about, their pace was perfect for me.

I'd been keen to get out for a run with Katherine since she had first come to my clinic. Katherine was nervous about her running capabilities, she'd joined a local running club and initially as the newbie she'd found herself at the back of the group, which she understood, but as the months continued and she was no longer the newby but still near the back, doubts were filling her mind and it was impacting her enjoyment of running. She'd come to my clinic telling me the progress of the others, but not acknowledging her own path of accomplishments.

During her massage sessions, I'd bring the conversation back to her Whys – Katherine ran to be a good role model for her girls, she ran because she enjoyed how it made her feel, which was strong and proud (when she was not comparing herself to others).

Today we chatted about mental strength and self-belief.

I explained that I was not a fast runner and that my pace, which was comfortable for all three of us, was a pace that would probably never win a race, but was taking me on an extraordinary running adventure. I spoke about my Whys and the level of determination and persistence it was taking for me to keep going. These were the things that I wanted both Katherine and Geeta to take away from our run together.

I also knew that everything I was saying to them, I was re-iterating to myself – as well as being the athlete who was running these marathons every day, I was also my own mental coach and I had to listen, take on board and implement the advice I was giving. It was pretty good advice and came from a lot of experience.

I had a short time between my next lot of friends joining me, so I cruised around the lakes of Watermead letting the memories of my past drift in.

Lovely memories of the people I'd coached, encouraged and inspired to move their butts and look after their physical health. As well as me bellowing out exercise instructions 'run, burpee, run, crawl, press up, jump, c'mon you can do it', I'd also talk through their beliefs that they could do more than they thought and encourage them to find the depths to their determination.

Another two friends, Rekha Patel and Eleanor Lloyd Jones joined me just before I hit that magic halfway point.

I mentioned previously that I had set up a PledgeSport page to help fund this adventure. The funding structure I used was for individuals to donate an amount of money in return for thanks, books, t-shirts and the like. I also had an offer for companies to invest. I was a relatively unknown ultrarunner (I still am really) and while I asked many companies if they would like to invest in me and my adventure, only one company did and that was Unique Window Systems Ltd, the company owned by the husband of one of my massage clients, Rekha Patel. I was truly grateful in her belief in me, this money helped pay for the running shoes that I wore out – which was a total of five pairs by the end of the adventure.

El was one of my original lifelines during my 7in7 and one of the people I'd trained throughout my time as a coach. She has a quiet, yet steely determination. Once she set her mind to do something, she'd then get on with it, bit by bit, never complaining, just going through the experience. At each milestone she'd smile, accept the cheers and then put her head down and work on the next phase. I loved this about her.

El and Rekha kept me company as the kilometres clicked to that magic half marathon/half adventure total and as it did, we stopped, high fived, took some happy snaps, and I checked in with myself. My body was doing okay, my mind was thinking strong, my friends were doing fine – it was time to get the second half of this ma-hoosive adventure underway, and off we trotted.

I ended up finishing the last 15kms of the day on my own, but that was okay. I was getting very used to spending the time alone with my head. I had a job to do and I was going to do it.

Never give up. Never give in.

DAY 33. GRANTHAM CANAL, NOTTINGHAMSHIRE

Thursday 28th September, 2017

Daily distance: 43.4km

Time taken: 6hrs 16mins

Total adventure distance: 1414.1km

The evening before, I'd received a text from Dirk's wife Jane, asking if I'd run by theirs and take Dirk out for short run along the River Trent, he was still a bit stiff and sore from Sunday's Nottingham marathon and figured a little shuffle with me would do the trick.

Dirk was in fine fettle when I ran to his house and was still on a high from finishing the marathon, and so he should have been, he'd only trained to do a half and had somehow pulled a full marathon out of the bag. I checked in on his chaffed nipples - they were healing nicely.

We ran along the river giggling at our memories from when I had first arrived in the UK and the parties we'd had.

It was much of the same that we'd reminisced about on Sunday, short term memory loss is another symptom of the disease, but these conversations made Dirk smile and laugh and this, he explained, was his best way of winning his days.

'Look for a reason to smile, and then do it', Dirk said. It was simple.

I knew that I was out here to run a marathon, but I figured I had some spare time to sit for a bit. We sat on the River Trent's edge and watched the bird life floating by and smiled.

I dropped Dirk at his local gym in time for his yoga class and I headed back to my familiar canal paths, checking in with 'my' mama and papa swans and their babies. I smiled.

DAY 34. BRADGATE PARK & BEACON HILL, LEICESTERSHIRE

Friday 29th September, 2017

Daily distance: 43.3km

Time taken: 6hrs 28mins

Total adventure distance: 1457.4km

Day 34 was the start of getting the show back on the road for what was now going to be my longest stint away from home.

I was heading to Leicester with the fluid plan of running around more of my old training grounds and being joined by friends for little bits throughout the day. Sharif was finishing his working week before starting his annual leave, packing the van and coming to collect me in the early evening. Then together we would pootle off in Stan the Van to South Wales.

I parked my car at Willis's, which he kindly offered to babysit for the next two weeks, and with Rufus in tow, I shuffled off towards Bradgate Park to meet my first run-buddy of the day.

A tall gazelle of a man, Richard Thompson, came bounding along the road as I made my way to the country park's entrance. Richard was a sports massage client of mine and an awesome ultrarunner with legs that pretty much went as high as my belly button.

Richard's first comment to me was 'Geez Nikki, you've lost a lot of weight.' It was true, I had lost about 4kg in weight, but my body shape had also changed. I've always had muscular legs, but I always seemed to carry my excess bodyfat on my upper thighs making them look chunky (definitely not ballerina-svelte-like).

However, during this adventure the muscle content of my legs had increased whilst the bodyfat content had decreased (I had scales that took these measurements), and thus my legs were looking pretty darn good in my eyes.

Despite my legs looking more muscularly defined, they were still much shorter than Richard's and it seemed I was taking three strides to his one. I had to ask him to drop back to what was practically running on the spot for him so that we could run together for the short time he was with me. Thankfully he didn't mind.

At the other end of the Country Park I said so-long to Richard. I watched as his long legs finally got the opportunity to stride out and I thought I'd probably have to take five steps to his every one when he was in full run-mode. Looking back down to my own legs, I acknowledged that I was genuinely proud of them. They may have been short, but they sure could take me on amazing adventures.

Tamsin and Ben lived nearby here and that was my next stop to drop Rufus off for the next couple of weeks. I was going to miss my little girl, but I knew that she'd be spoilt with runs around this beautiful part of the world in the company of the Robinson family. I am so thankful that they love and adore her as much as I do.

Another client and friend, Sharon Rassool, had let me know she was around and about today and would love a little bit of a jog with me. This worked quite nicely, she lived a good distance away to get some miles in, with a little added bonus of also being just down the road from a gorgeous little place *The Café Next Door* where another friend, Helen Riley, worked and she had let me know that there was a coffee and a huge piece of cake with my name on it waiting for me. I will literally run anywhere for cake.

Although I knew this area extremely well, it was my local run-training haunt, I let Sharon take over the direction control with just one little request – could we avoid all the massive hills in the area, which proved to be easier said than done.

As we ran, I noticed we were heading towards Beacon Hill, of which I made mention, but Sharon promised she knew another route around the hill that didn't have a big climb. As the trail got steeper, Sharon said that it wasn't quite the way she remembered it, and acknowledged that yes it was a little steep around here Nikki, as I panted my way to the highest point in Leicestershire.

Of course, it was worth it though. The trail was indeed one I hadn't run before and the lookout point that allowed us to scan the skyline of the City of Leicester, Loughborough and 26.2 ish miles away, the City of Nottingham, was simply stunning.

Sharon did point out that it was all downhill from here back to hers, which was my finish line for the day and off we trotted.

Sharif arrived at Sharon's about the same time as we did. The day was done, the van was packed, and we were ready to roll.

I mentioned that my relationship with Sharif was fairly new, we had met on 1st March 2017, St David's Day, and it had gone from 'let's meet for a coffee' to 'let's travel the length and breadth of the UK in a van whilst I chase a seven year dream goal', all in the space of 5 months. I had met his daughters before we took off on this adventure, but I had yet to meet his parents as they lived in South Wales. That was about to change as that's where we were heading next.

This Aussie gal's running tour of the UK was about to run through the land of leeks, daffodils and dragons.

DAY 35. TAFF TRAIL & CARDIFF, GLAMORGAN

Saturday 30th September, 2017

Daily distance: 42.8km

Time taken: 6hrs 17mins

Total adventure distance: 1500.2km

We arrived in Penarth, Wales at the home of Sharif's folks, Sue and Feroze Owadally, around 9pm.

Although I'd had a shower at Sharon's before leaving Leicester, in an attempt to at least look a bit presentable to meet his parents for the first time, it was a pretty wasted effort. I had snoozed during the three-hour drive and I had awoken looking and feeling somewhat like a starving zombie.

Thankfully Sharif had forewarned his mum of my current state of being and she had prepared a lot of food for when we arrived.

Sue and Feroze were absolutely lovely and welcomed me into their home (and kitchen) with open arms, but I dread to think what they thought of me, a dishevelled, exhausted, hungry wreck.

I ate as I was being introduced, I ate as they tried to get their head around what I was doing, and I ate as I headed up to bed.

Sharif explained to his folks that I was waking up in the middle of the night eager to eat everything that I could lay my hands on, so taking a plate of food upstairs with me was the best way to cope with my midnight munchies. I was eating again, breakfast, when Sharif's mum woke and joined us for coffee.

It was a Saturday, which gave us the opportunity for another Parkrun start - Grangemoor Parkrun.

Sue drove us to the start and along the way asked where she should pick us up. No need, I'd run back. She pointed out that there was a perfectly good bus service that I could be using 'Yep, but where would the fun in that be?' I responded.

Sue later told me that she thought maybe I had a warped sense of the word fun. She may be right.

Arriving on time for this Parkrun, my goal was to stay ahead of the tail-walker, which I managed … just.

After a quick chat with the Grangemoor running locals, it was decided that my best tack for the day was to run along the 55-mile Taff trail which ran alongside the lush River Taff. And to my surprise and delight it was going to take me to a place I'd always wanted to visit.

Whilst Sharif had a deep connection with Wales, he was born there, I too had a connection with South Wales. My business outside of shorts, is a rental property company and the bulk of my company's rental properties are located in the valleys of South Wales. Castell Coch is a fairy-tale turret castle built on the side of a hill, nestled in amongst the beech woods of Fforest Fawr and I must have driven past it hundreds of times with the thought of one day I'll take a closer look at that. Today was going to be that day, for as it turned out it was pretty much the exact distance I had to run to be my turnaround point for an out and back along the Taff Trail.

I think I've mentioned this once or twice before about castles – their original purpose being to provide a safe and elevated vantage point for the castle occupants to look out over their land – well Castell Coch is a little different, in that it is a folly, built by the 3rd Marquis of Bute in the 1870's, as a summer getaway. Notwithstanding, it's still built on a bloody big hill, and as we ran towards it, leaving the river and the trail heading up and up and up, I realised that perhaps today was not going to be the day that I knocked on its door and had a little nosey around. Halfway up the hill, I was happy enough to see it close enough from there.

Back down on the trail, I cruised back into the heart of Cardiff where an abundance of ice-cream vendors more than made up for the 'close but no cigar' visit to Castell Coch.

As the kilometres clicked down to done, the drizzle began. Come on Nikki, just a little bit further, my mind chant began, but there was another noise coming from outside of my mind. Sharif was suggesting I run to the end of the Penarth Pier 'it'll be a great photo opportunity' he suggested.

I guess so, but it was wet, the wind was picking up, it was all the way down there and I was all the way down here. 'Just do it' he said, as he gave me a little push on the back.

I shuffled along the pier feeling the weather roll in and as my GPS's clicked to 42.2kms I noticed a woman crazy-waving and whooping at me. Sharif had organised Charlotte Spencer, my very first friend in the UK, to meet us at the end of the pier.

And she had beer, a chocolate medal and a cake that she'd iced with the words 'you fit wanker' on it … this was indeed a wonderful photo opportunity and worth being wind-blown and drenched at the end of the Penarth pier.

Where? my head ponders
My feet take flight to wander
New paths of wonder

~ Nikki Love

WEEK 6

DAY 36. ST DAVIDS, PEMBROKESHIRE

Sunday 1ˢᵗ October, 2017

Daily distance: 42.2km

Time taken: 6hrs 20mins

Total adventure distance: 1542.4km

We had a three-hour drive from Penarth to St David's for marathon 36. This meant that we had an extremely early morning rise, this also meant that Miss Grumpy Pants was tagging along for the ride. Sharif suggested I drop the seat back and get a little more sleep, I think it was as much for his good as mine.

Sharif woke me as we arrived at St David's, it was time to get me going but first we needed to pick up some extra supplies — water being the necessity and chocolate being my craving. The shopkeeper gave a little whoop, my story was in the local newspaper that he'd just finished reading and he recognised me.

We had a little chat about the adventure so far and he gave a proud shoutout to his hometown, St David's. He was certain I was going to love running around the area, and to get us off to a great start he gave us the water for free.

St David's Cathedral was going to be today's start and finish line with a lot of coastal path running in between. Sharif shared a piece of Catholic history with me — Pope Calixtus II wrote a papel bull decreeing that two pilgrimages to St David's was the equivalent to one pilgrimage to the Vatican.

I had been to the Vatican and I was now at St David's, so I was hoping that both these visits would add up to a good omen for me and perhaps the weather for the day, which had been windy, wet and fairly miserable up to this point. Maybe it would clear by the time I hit the coastal path.

I was tired, but felt I was running along quite nicely until I saw something ahead.

'Eek', I shouted to Sharif, who was riding alongside. 'Did you see that?'

'What?' he answered nonplussed.

Apparently, he didn't see the huge cat thing, that I'd just seen run across the road and into the bushes.

I was adamant I saw a big cat, not a house cat, it was like a huge jungle cat. 'Do mountain lions live in Wales, or Tasmanian tigers, or was there an escaped leopard on the loose?' I shrieked.

Sharif took the lead whilst I followed behind, my eyes frantically darting from the road to the bushes and back to the road. Maybe I was a little more tired than I originally thought and was now hallucinating. This was going to be a long day.

Sharif was particularly looking forward to getting onto the coastal path. That first night we had met we talked about the Wales Coast Path and how he wanted to run the entire length of it as an adventure. He figured it would probably take him a couple of years of a weekend here and a weekend there of running a bit at a time to get it done.

At the time I did question why he hadn't contemplated doing it all in one go and maybe I may have goaded him and unfairly questioned his masculinity for not considering it … banter and such. He pointed out that most 'normal' people didn't run for weeks or months at a time. I nodded and took his comments on board, and responded back 'Why be normal?' I think he fell in love with me right there and then (maybe?).

At some point within the months of meeting him and starting this adventure, his thoughts of what 'normal' was, had been turned upside down. Running for weeks and months at a time could be normal, well it was becoming our normal. As we headed towards the coastal path, he mentioned that I'd now left him no option than to plan to take on his Run Around Wales in one go ... damn me and my weird normal.

I started an apology, but he cut me short saying don't be stupid – he loved that I'd warped his mind as to what normal was, he loved being a part of making this stooopid adventure a reality and he loved that he was now considering doing his Run Around Wales in one go – together we'd make that a reality too.

To say he was a bit disappointed with the path was a slight under-statement. The trodden part of the path was not much wider than my single foot, which meant I had to keep my eyes on where I was putting said foot each and every step. This stretch of the Wales Coast path was okay for walking (at a push), it was difficult for running, but on a bike (as Sharif currently was) it was treacherous.

This set Sharif off. Sharif is proudly Welsh, but he had some pretty strong views about the competencies of the Welsh government, and he was letting me know what he thought of their spending.

The Welsh government had spent a fortune on signing the Wales Coast Path and to be fair, the signage was top notch. The path it was signposting however, could perhaps have received a small share of the finances to make it a little more user friendly in some places. That was my impartial view.

It was slow going along the path and as much as I had liked the idea that I would run along it for as far as possible, at the current pace I was stumbling along and with Sharif having to carry the bike instead of riding it, the day was going to take forever. We needed to find a detour off the path.

Changing tack, we wandered through a farm which we think had a right of way access path through it (if not, sorry to the farm owner) and eventually found a quiet country lane which helped me get back into a running rhythm again.

It also helped that Sharif said that this quiet country lane would take us to a beach which could possibly have a shop with ice-cream. I was sold, and with a little bit of extra help from my playlist, we headed towards the beach of Whitesands Bay.

I'd discovered that I liked having my music blaring beside me, rather than through headphones directly into my ears. Listening to music this way, with it surrounding me, I'm still able to hear traffic and I can also sing and jig about.

Sharif was getting good at choosing the songs that would add a bit of pep to my step.

In particular, 'Proud Mary' by Ike & Tina Turner was a favourite. It starts off slow telling a little story about how 'we never ever like to do things nice and easy; we like to do things nice and rough'.

This was the story of this adventure. We were most certainly not doing anything nice and easy. It was rough, but my goodness, it was fun.

We did a live Facebook stream whilst Sharif was playing some music to get me moving a little faster. I was rundancing which is a combination of my feet moving in a running motion, with the occasional skip, jump or side movement to accentuate a phrase in the song, and my arms doing some form of armography that tries to keep time with the music whilst keeping my balance running.

Stealers Wheel's song 'Stuck in the middle with you' was playing and the line 'clowns to the left of me, jokers to the right' was absolutely tickling my funny bone. Sharif was trying to film me, get some sense out of me and I was singing this chorus at the top of my voice and giggling my head off. He was the clown to the left of me, I pointed out to the world of Facebook. Still makes me laugh as I think back on it. Even more when I watch the footage. Captured forever.

As with all my days these past couple of weeks, I was running okay, but the distance between 25-35kms was becoming my daily hurdle to get over - I'd lose momentum and focus, I'd stop and fiddle about with my backpack, then re-start and then stop and fiddle some more, and I'd go into a little bit of a funk. Just a little bit.

I knew what I was there to do, and I sure as hell knew I was going to keep going but I'd have this daily little slump in which the difficulty of the challenge became a point of focus.

Each day I would try and take my head and my eyes elsewhere rather than focus on the distance ticking down ever so slowly.

Similar to the swallows I'd seen at Rutland Water, I'd started noticing congregations of big black crows. The more rural I was, the more crows I'd see, and like the swallows, they'd get a bit uppity and noisy late afternoon – usually when I was hitting my 30km point.

As I ran past a village church, I watched a murder of crows rise up into the air, swoosh about, go back to the trees and repeat over and over again. It was noisy, beautiful if not somewhat eerie - both the collective name for a group of crows as well as the location – my tired mind kept flashing scenes from Hitchcock's movie *The Birds* as my tired legs struggled to shuffle me away.

We passed a sign for potatoes and trying to keep me entertained, Sharif told me a joke.

Three blokes – an Englishman, a Welshman and an Irishman were on the run from the police. They'd escaped into the farmlands but were being tracked down. 'Quick!' said the Welshman, as they scurried into a barn. 'Here's 3 sacks. Climb inside and hide.' They each climbed inside and waited as the police surrounded the barn and then moved inside.

Noticing the sacks, they decided to kick each one to see what was inside. They kicked the first sack that contained the Englishman. The Englishman responded with a 'mooooo'. The police figured there was nothing there to see other than a sack of cows. They kicked the second sack that had the Welshman in it. He responded with a 'baaaaa'. 'Nothing to see here either, other than a sack of sheep', said the policemen. They kicked the last sack that had the Irishman in it, and he responded with 'potatoes' … and the police nabbed him.

It had us both in stitches. This is what happens when you're tired and pushing extremes. You start hallucinating that you can see jungle cats roaming around in the bushes, that murders of crows are going to attack and that Irish potato jokes are the funniest thing in the world.

Whitesands Bay was ace. It's amazing how the noise of waves crashing onto a shoreline can sooth and calm me, I ran up to the shallows and took a few minutes to take it all in. I love the beach and I wanted to stop and have a swim, have an ice-cream and spend the rest of the day watching the waves roll in, but that wasn't what I'd signed up for. This was a two-month commitment to run a marathon every day and I still had a ways go today.

Instead, I attempted a cartwheel. It was about midway through the cartwheel that I realised I hadn't used my arms for anything more than balance and to put food in my mouth for the past 36 days. I collapsed into a giggling heap on the sand and vowed to work on my arms once this adventure was over. Being able to cartwheel is equally as important as being able to run.

We made it back to St David's as the daylight was starting to fade. The shopkeeper had been spot on, I loved running around this area – I'd eaten ice-cream, I'd been on a beach, I'd giggled like a giggly thing and most likely because I had been to both the Vatican and now to St David's, the weather had cleared and it ended up being a beautiful autumn day.

Sue had baked a home-made chicken pie for our dinner, and it was sitting waiting for us when we eventually got in.

I was so very tired, I was a dishevelled mess who really needed a shower, but I was also so extremely hungry so I went directly to the kitchen table and, doing my utmost to keep my face out of my plate, shovelled in as much food as I could. I'm not really sure what his mum was thinking about this woman that her son had dragged (quite literally) into her house but I was just too tired to worry about trying to make a good first impression.

DAY 37. PENARTH, GLAMORGAN

Monday 2nd October, 2017

Daily distance: 43.4km

Time taken: 6hrs 30mins

Total adventure distance: 1585.8km

We'd intended to head out to the west of Wales again and run at a place called Rhossili, but that meant a four hour round driving trip and an extra early morning start and Sharif would have to put up with grumpy morning Nikki and we'd get home late and my period had started through the night and we were going to be on the road until day 50 and all the 'ands' kept stacking until it made sense to stay local and enjoy the Owadally's home comforts for as long as possible.

The alternative route Sharif set me was to head to the town of Barry, a coastal town best known for its seaside fair and the TV programme Gavin and Stacey – which was lost on me having never watched it, but I was told it was funny. Notwithstanding my lack of Gavin and Stacey knowledge, I was quite looking forward to seeing Barry – it had a beachfront.

It was a fairly simple out and back route along the main road between Penarth and Barry and all was going okay. I say okay, I was having problems with my tummy, the diarrhoea that comes along with my period was problematic and I had to keep finding friendly shops and garages that had toilets, but apart from that it was going okay … until it wasn't.

I'd been running along the footpath by the side of the road until the footpath ran out which happened to be at a particularly gnarly bit of road that had consecutive hairpin bends and very little grass verge.

I was tired, hormonal, emotional, drained.

I'd managed to get around the first bend, hoping that the road would become easier but it didn't and I ended up standing on the grass on the blind bend watching cars zoom by me in both directions not really sure what to do. The few times I attempted to run a few steps along the road were scary and I was tooted, not in a friendly 'hey runner, congratulations and keep up the good work' kind of way, I was being tooted in a 'get off the bloody road you crazy woman' kind of way.

My brain was not functioning. I couldn't quite work out how to move – forward or backward.

The only solution I could think of was to call Sharif and cry. I explained how I was stuck and that I didn't know which way to run. Cool and calm as usual, he told me to wait where I was, and he'd get there shortly.

I stood and cried and watched the cars speed by me for what felt like an eternity (it was perhaps 15 minutes) - thankfully Sharif had been out shopping with his mum when I called, and as they were on their way back home it didn't take long for them to drive to where I'd got stuck.

Parking up on the side of the road just before where the footpath had ended, Sharif phoned me and managed to give me traffic advice that helped me get back around the hairpin bend and I eventually traipsed back on the grass verge to safety.

The tears were full on now. I was sobbing my heart out. It really didn't warrant this flood of tears. However, coming to a standstill, being so tired and not being able to keep running forward was too much for me to bear. I must have looked a right state, as the tears streamed.

My logic was blocked, and I wailed at Sharif – nothing was going right, everything was going wrong, I couldn't do this, it was all too much. He held me in his arms and listened to my hysterics until I calmed down.

All I had to do was to run back the way I had come and then go off on another path, even if it was around the block of his parent's house a million times, to get to the full marathon distance. He knew that I knew it too, it just took me a bit of time to get there.

It occurred to me, quite a while later in the day mind you, that Sharif's mum had sat in the car watching me have a little meltdown and I again wondered what she must have thought about this woman her son had found.

It was my second New Year's Eve with Sharif, post the 63 marathon adventure and many more low key and less hysterical visits to Penarth that the topic of what Sharif's parents had thought of me during that first visit came up. As we toasted in the new year, Sharif's Aunty Theresa said that Sue had thought I was completely nuts which as far as she was concerned made me perfect for her son.

I'll take that. Phew.

DAY 38. PEN Y FAN & BRECON, POWYS

Tuesday 3rd October, 2017

Daily distance: 42.6km

Time taken: 7hrs 5mins

Total adventure distance: 1628.4km

We had put a request out on Facebook for any locals around the Brecon area to advise us on a route that incorporated the local mountain, Pen Y Fan. I was keen to go up at least one high altitude during my marathons and as Pen Y Fan is the highest point in the south of the UK, today was going to be my 'high' day.

Becca Jones had been watching my runs on social media, and she offered to meet us in the morning – she had the perfect route for us. She'd been telling her two young sons about me and what I was doing, and they were keen to meet someone who was attempting a world record. Unfortunately, Ewan was at school, but her youngest son, Iolo, was still pre-school age and so joined his mum and met us in Brecon. The plan was to leave the van in Brecon, Becca would drive us to our start location at the base of Pen Y Fan and we'd run back.

On the short drive to our start, 4-year-old Iolo shared his Guinness World Record ambitions with us. With conviction, wispy and fair-haired Iolo declared that he wanted to be the world's hairiest man! Aim high young man, aim high.

Becca dropped us at a stunning but quite secluded location and pointed out the sheep/walking track that we were going to take to get to the top of the Pen Y Fan. It was not the main thorough-fare up the mountain, the main thoroughfare is pathed, and you can't see the top of Pen Y Fan from the car park. You climb up and over a few hills before climbing the final up to the top – it's a comfortable steepness over a comfortable distance for most walkers.

From where we were, you could always see the tippy top of Pen Y Fan, basically because the path we were heading towards prac-tically went directly up the rock face of the mountain. I thought this might be a good thing being able to see the apex of my climb, but as we started going up and the minutes became the first hour which surprisingly quickly became the second, and I hadn't even made it to the halfway point, I realised that I may have over-egged my ambition.

After three hours I had covered a measly five kilometres in actual distance – it was at this point I realised that this may not have been one of my smartest ideas.

We had to make a decision, I could keep struggling upwards to get a 'top of the mountain' photo, which was more a vanity thing than a purpose to my day thing. The purpose of my day was to run a marathon, and if I started the descent and headed back into Brecon where I was going to finish running along the river, a nice flat river, then I stood more chance of achieving my goal of finish-ing by 5pm.

There was a good reason for finishing by 5pm, Sharon Copson had kindly offered to give me a complimentary massage and it would have been darn rude of me to be late and in the bigger picture scheme of things accepting a massage to help my legs keep me going to the end of this adventure rather than get a 'top of a mountain' photo was a wiser choice.

The summit was going to have to wait for another day.

Going down was bliss.

Arriving back in Brecon, Sharif switched from running with me to riding up ahead and using the incentive of a massage to get to, to urge me on and get some speed into my running. I think I actually did that thing called a negative split – my second marathon half was faster than my first and dare I say it, the river part of my run was also bliss.

Becca met us again at the end of the day with some locally sourced and truly divine chocolate treats. It was just what I needed to complete the Wales part of this adventure - chocolate cake and a massage.

Tomorrow we were heading back across the border to the southern parts of England.

Using the power of social media again, Sharif had managed to organise another complimentary massage from Stephanie Blake who was based in Portishead, so Portishead was where we were heading.

DAY 39. PORTISHEAD, SOMERSET

Wednesday 4th October, 2017

Daily distance: 42.9km

Time taken: 6hrs 48mins

Total adventure distance: 1671.3km

We hadn't worked out a specific route for today's marathon. On the map we'd noticed that there was a coastal path, a few nature reserves and some woods around and about – basically we were just going to wing it and simply make sure I ran 42.2kms.

Wanting to make sure that everything was going to be hunky dory for the end of the day, Sharif popped into the clinic where Stephanie worked to let her know our plans, which set off a lovely chain of events.

Sharif met the clinic's receptionist Kyle. Kyle noticed Sharif's t-shirt with the 63 marathons details emblazoned on the back. Kyle realised that I was running 63 marathons. It just so happened that Kyle was the partner, he's now the husband, of the amazing ultrarunner Ben Smith, who had run 401 marathons in 401 days. What a wonderful coincidence. Kyle asked if we'd like to meet Ben at the end of day when I'd be back for my massage. Yes, indeed I would!

We set off, me running, Sharif on the bike, towards the coastal path with rather big smiles on our faces. I was hoping to get some advice from an experienced ultrarunner, and we were both going to meet someone we had admired from afar.

The coastal path was yet again another path that provided stunning vantage points of the British coastline, but was extremely narrow in sections, overgrown in others and rough, rugged and extremely tree-rooty for most of it.

Whilst I would normally love to run along paths like this when I had fresh legs, I had not possessed a set of fresh legs since way back in week one of this adventure so the technicality of this path was slowing me down to even slower than my normal slow. As for Sharif, he moaned, cursed and had to carry the bike quite a few times – it was not his favourite path.

I'm glad we persevered to its end, it led us to a stunning woodland that had wide paths and was a joy to run around. We took a quick vote - two to none - to not go back along the coastal path and instead use the abundance of cycle routes in the area which took us along quiet country lanes, through quaint English villages and eventually back to the nature reserve in Portishead.

Eager to make it back to the clinic on time, I'd slightly misjudged the distance again and so began my mini circling pattern game of 'ring-a-ring-o'-roses' and around and around the block of the clinic I ran – I think today's loop count was five.

I'd got used to running little loops to finish and it's not the worst way to finish a marathon, but today's loop involved me running past a fish and chip shop that was getting ready for its evening service. Ooooh the smell. I wanted – no I *needed* some fish and chips – but they were going to have to wait until after these loops, after my massage, and after meeting one of my ultra-running heroes, Ben Smith … I desperately hoped they wouldn't sell out.

Stephanie was ready and waiting and provided my body with the most wonderful massage. She had helped look after Ben's body during his gargantuan adventure, so she knew what I needed.

As Ben came into the clinic, I think Sharif and I actually tussled to get to him first for a great big hug. I had so many questions, Sharif was just being a big fangirl.

Hugs given equally to both Sharif and me, I then set about picking Ben's brain, my first and obvious question was – when did it get easier? As I mentioned, Ben had done 401 marathons, surely he knew a thing or two about how tough I was finding it.

He shared three tips with me, that I'll share with you for when you fancy doing something crazy like this … yes?

1. Eat more food.
2. Stop for lunch and a pint (and don't stress about the time it takes to complete a marathon).
3. It gets easier after marathon 50.

Ben shared that from marathon fifty he stopped trying to follow an 'ideal' way of running a marathon - trying to eat only healthy foods and run a certain marathon time. Instead at marathon 50, he began eating more of what he fancied and often stopping for lunch and a mid-marathon cider, figuring that this way he would enjoy his adventure more. He had an entire year, and then some, to get through and he didn't want to struggle miserably for the whole of that time.

Oky doky, all valid points, I had started stressing that people might laugh at the length of time my marathons were taking me – I was getting them done and that was all that mattered.

I knew I needed to eat more food because I had been waking up in the middle of the night starving and always looking for more food. Sharif was dealing with this by making sure he put a plate of food (generally some form of meat) by the side of the bed for, as he described it, my midnight-gremlin-snack-attack. I'd sit up in bed and start hoeing down on food, and watch out for your fingers if you got in the way between me and my plate of food.

The idea of a beer mid-way was novel, but hey, Ben was an expert, and I was willing to give it a go.

I'd just finished marathon 39, I still had a little way to go to get to marathon 50 and that feeling of it getting easier, but it was on the horizon … good, good.

I thanked Ben for sharing his tips and for coming in to visit, it really had perked me up and strengthened my resolve that I could do this crazy adventure.

From Portishead we had a bit of a drive to do, but first I needed those fish and chips that I'd been drooling over during the final twenty minutes of my run. Ben, the sweetheart that he is, shouted us our fish supper and Sharif and I sat in the back of the van, big smiles on our faces, devouring every morsel of the meal that our new ultrarunner hero friend had bought us.

Sharif drove to our next destination Braunton, where we were staying with my friends Helen and Anton Poll. Helen had let us know that she'd prepared dinner for us – was I hungry? Indeed, I was Helen, and this became the first of my double dinners that we implemented into my daily routine.

My end of marathon routine became - get a can of San Pellegrino Limonata (it really was a craving I was having and it had to be this specific drink) and either a donut or a cake snack into me. Shortly after, have a meal such as fish and chips or a pie and chips, or roast chicken drumsticks or thighs. Sharif would then drive to our next location where we'd have dinner.

I liked being told to eat more.

DAY 40. BRAUNTON, DEVON

Thursday 5th October, 2017

Daily distance: 42.9km

Time taken: 6hrs 2mins

Total adventure distance: 1714.2km

Today I had the pleasure of Helen's company, she was chief in charge of navigation to make sure I didn't get lost, motivation and conversation to keep me focussed and running, and café scouting to keep us both fuelled with enough caffeine and cake to get through 42.2kms.

We were heading out along the Tarka Trail – thankfully, it turned out, not the hilly way. I'd run parts of this trail during previous surf and run escapes to the region and the parts of the trail that I knew well hugged the surf coast and took in many a rolling hill that Devonshire was renowned for. Instead, Helen was taking me the flat way from Braunton to Bideford and back.

First things first though, Helen had two little munchkins, Lottie and Martha, to take to school, so our day started with the parenting job of the 'school run'. Helen and the girls flew off on their bikes and I did my utmost to keep up running behind.

As well as dropping the girls at school, I'd also been invited by the Head to host the morning assembly - today's topic of talk was comparing their day to mine. I shared that my day was to start running at 9am, though today I'd started a little earlier, there was no way I wasn't including the school run into my total distance. I'd then keep running whilst they were in class, whilst they were on their lunchbreak and even beyond when they'd finish at 3pm … yep I'd probably run until 5pm. Getting the students to then do a little maths equation, we also worked out that their school running track was approximately 400m long, meaning that I'd have to run 105 and a bit times around it to equate to 42.2kms. These comparisons blew their minds. To tell the truth, it blew my mind every single day too, but not wanting to think too much about it (I was better at the doing rather than thinking of doing), we all headed out and had a little run about on their track – and yes I counted these running steps into my day too.

As we pootled along the path, me running and Helen cycling, a couple of ladies headed towards us from the opposite direction. As they got close, Helen realised it was her mum. Helen's mum had been following me on Facebook and had hoped to find us out here. She'd been inspired to get out and do her steps every day as she watched me turn up in different parts of the country and 'run my little heart out', as she put it.

I knew that I was getting a lot of views on Facebook, and I was receiving lovely comments from a regular crowd, but I was always surprised to hear that people outside of my normal circle were watching and that they were getting something out of it too.

Sometimes, usually during the 25-35km part of my day when I'd have a mood dip and a grump, I'd wonder why I was doing this. I knew there was the money raising aspect but hearing that I was inspiring people to get up, get out and get active was an added extra bonus and simply a lovely piece of information to receive.

That evening I had a phone call from another new friend, Andy Vandenberg, who had been watching my adventure and had been inspired to up-the-anti on his own challenge. He'd set himself the goal of running 52 marathons in a year but had fallen behind his target and as a means to catch up he thought he'd give running seven marathons in seven days a go. Sharif and Andy had been coordinating schedules and we were going to be in the same place at the same time for his 6th and my 47th marathon. During our conversation that evening he asked me for some tips – I passed on the information I'd been given from Ben as well as the stuff I'd learned and said 'eat, mate, eat, eat, eat, oh and make sure you pack a tub of Vaseline, chaffing during my first week had been a bitch'.

Hopefully it would make the seven days he was about to embark on a little easier.

DAY 41. LAUNCESTON, CORNWALL

Friday 6th October, 2017

Daily distance: 42.8km

Time taken: 7hrs 26mins

Total adventure distance: 1757km

Rather than drive off last night and sleep in the van, we had opted to enjoy the comfort of the Poll's hospitality for a second night. It was a good call, but it did mean leaving in the wee small hours of the morning to get to today's location of Launceston, 50 miles away.

Now I may have mentioned once or twice (or perhaps a gadjillion times) that I'm not a morning person and 'Little Miss Grumpy-pants' tends to be in charge until about 8am (although Sharif will probably tell you it's more like 9 or 10am) but finding an upside to circumstances, and there is always an upside if you look hard enough, is a wonderful habit to practice.

The upside of today's early start was that I was able to wrap myself up in my new Dryrobe jacket that I had been gifted from the head of the company, Gideon Bright. He was a friend of Helen and Anton's; his children went to the primary school I'd visited, and he simply loved the story of what I was doing. If you don't know what a Dryrobe is, then please do go and check out the photo library that I've put together to accompany this book and you'll know why I felt all warm and fuzzy about my Dryrobe, better still, go and check out their website … I digress, I loved curling up into my new robe and catching a few more zzzz's as Sharif drove us to Launceston.

My start and finish location was the Launceston Tesco supermarket, and whilst Sharif headed in to ask for permission to park the van for the day and to grab some food stuffs, I shuffled around in the back of the van to get myself ready for the day, my new comfy-robe/sleeping-bag/blanket was proving to be little too comfy, but I'd never get this marathon done if I didn't shimmy out of it. Robe discarded, shoes on, backpack filled with food and watches all finally ready to hit go, we headed off.

Today's run pretty much started with a steep hill down which meant only one thing, to get back to the van, I'd be finishing with a steep hill up, but I wasn't going to dwell too much on that, I had many hours to get through before then.

Careening down a hill is fun, so is people watching, and as I hurtled down, I caught a glimpse of someone outside painting their wall. Not only was she painting her wall, but she had also painted her face with a moustache, a beard and was creating a piece of art on the wall of her house, I had to stop and chat. We shared our stories, she was channelling Poirot and passionately painting her thoughts and feelings on the side of her house, I was channelling Forrest Gump and passionately running an adventure across the UK – we came to the conclusion that we were both perhaps a little bit eccentric but the world needed a bit of eccentricity, and that following your passion and purpose was a wonderful feeling to be had.

The main noise we heard throughout the morning was the birds, the bumblebees and me moaning about the hills – 'Where was my canal?'

There are no canals down south, just lots of country lanes and bicycle paths for me to run and Sharif to cycle along.

The moaning didn't last too long, it was actually a beautiful place to spend a day. The Devonshire countryside is stunning and the country lanes we ran along provided so many photo opportunities of the rolling green farmland and the coastline that came into view at the peak of every hill and, oh my goodness, there were a lot of hills. I did have trouble with the hills and had to walk up most of them, but for every up, there was a down and it was a thrill running down them.

I was working hard on the whole getting more calories into me and being in the southern UK region it seemed appropriate to consume the local calorific culinary delights of Cornish pasties and scones that Sharif had so wisely purchased that morning.

Another must-do in the south, and given that we were in cider country, was obviously to test and buy some cider. I ran past farm after farm of apple orchards and by mid-afternoon, with the sun blazing down on us, we decided to pop into an orchard with a shopfront for a taste test.

Holy moly, the sip I had nearly blew my socks off, this was some sweet and very potent apple juice. This was definitely going to have to be a post run drink or I'd never get through the afternoon run part of my run, and even at the end of the day, it was only ever going to be a sup, I'm not sure what the alcohol content was, but by golly it was strong.

Speaking of socks, I'd had some new Runderwear socks delivered to the Poll's house and whilst these hills were hurting my quads, my feet were having the time of their lives in their new coverings.

To say that my feet were in heaven may sound a little over the top, but that's exactly how they felt. From the very first time I slipped my tootsies into my Runderwear socks I discarded all the other socks from my life and I had bought other new socks specifically for this run – they subsequently stayed in a bag in the back of the van.

My feet, which had so far had carried me over 1000 miles up and down the length of the UK, were doing a happy dance - well a happy shuffle.

That hill back to the van, well I barely even noticed it and the now common loop around the car park to get to the magic 42.2 daily target - standard!

I wouldn't say it was getting easier, but the normality of it was.

DAY 42. LAND'S END, CORNWALL

Saturday 7th October, 2017

Daily distance: 42.7km

Time taken: 6hrs 54mins

Total adventure distance: 1799.7km

For anybody thinking of taking up the sport of ultra-running or more specifically ultra-running over multiple weeks, living out of a van and travelling long distances each night (or early morning) to get to a different start location in a different part of the country, here's a little word of warning – it is not a glamorous sport, but …

I'll get to the 'but' in a minute, first let me just describe the night to morning experience.

We had a long haul from Launceston to Mousehole (ain't Mousehole the cutest name for a little town – by the way it's not pronounced 'mouse hole', its pronounced 'Mosel', but where's the fun in that? I obviously ignored the proper pronunciation and called it Mouse Hole all day) and along the way, the fair weather turned foul, and it started to rain.

We arrived at a campsite in the dark and rain and the last thing I wanted to do was head to the outside shower block and have a shower, instead I stayed grimy from the day's efforts.

Despite not going for a shower, I still had to get up and get out of the van and head out into the rain many times throughout the night with my dodgy belly, yeah the diarrhoea was now such a part of my day that I wasn't mentioning it in my writing, but it was still there.

I cried, I had night hot flushes (bloody perimenopause), I fidgeted in the confined space of Stan the van and by the time morning arrived, I was knackered and looked a mess. Sharif hadn't fared much better, having to put up with me all night.

As I said, not a glamorous sport …

'But'

Having a purpose, a passion and a powerful WHY to put up with the short-term ugliness for long term gains is definitely worth it.

Today I had the company of John Yelland, who had got in touch with us because he too was a passionate campaigner and fund-raiser for the charity HDA.

Turns out we had something else in common. John's son was also called Riley, and as the run progressed we found out it was because both his wife, Ang, and I had loved the TV show *Buffy the Vampire Slayer* and one of the main characters of the show was Riley … small world of weird connections.

It was cold, wet and extremely windy, not the greatest of conditions to run in at the best of times, however I think John found it even harder as he had to slow down his pace to keep back at my pace, which was now entering sloth territory as the previous night's lack of sleep combined with the hills and the elements took their toll. John was a sweetheart and didn't complain, instead he battled on slightly ahead of me to try and create a little buffer against the elements.

Mid-morning, John had to say so long, he had the parenting duties of getting his Riley to football practice, as for me I had my furthest landmark south, Land's End, to get to.

I'd noticed some signs about a cycling event and before I knew it, I was in the thick of the Land's End Sportive 100.

Sharif had told me that the elevation today wasn't going to be as bad as yesterday's and to be fair, it wasn't, but there were a couple of killer hills.

One in particular was super steep, even with all the switchbacks it had. I was running down, watching the cyclists try and make their way up. I was having a tough old time out there, but these guys attempting to cycle up and into the driving wind and rain - I think I had it a little easier as I watched many a rider have to admit defeat and walk that hill. We exchanged pleasantries, as we passed. I obviously had a smile on my face on the way down, but I knew I'd be hauling my butt back up here later in the day. As for now, I did what I was now getting well practiced at doing, I let the thought of running back up the hill slide away to the back of my brain for laters.

I'd also become well practiced at thinking about my day in 5kms chunks, or a Parkrun. I split my day into Parkruns and at the start of each day I knew that I was going to do eight and a bit of them. The bit, well Sharif's coined phrase of 'you can fall the last bit' dealt with those - 2.2kms at the end was not that far to fall if I needed to.

These were the mental strategies that I was using – my head liked that eight was a small number and within each of those eight 5kms there were even more small numbers. I'd count down each 5km chunk as 5, 4, 3, 2, 1 and done. The other thought behind using a 5km chunk is that I know for certain that I can do a 5km - I had memories of having completed hundreds of them, and so each day I'd start off with 'I know I can do a 5km Parkrun, so let's go do this' and I would continue my day in this way.

It worked for me.

I was looking forward to visiting Land's End, as I'd only ever seen it from a distance. I'd peered out towards it during several surfing trips to Sennen, a little surf town further north along the coast, but I hadn't wanted to give up a day of surf to visit. Turns out it was a good choice.

Land's End was ummm, touristy-tacky, especially when compared with John O'Groats.

It seemed to be somewhat caught in the middle of a kids theme park and a living history centre, and what was most disappointing was that it had made its signpost, which twins the signpost at John O'Groats, a paid-for experience with fences surrounding it and somebody waiting to take a happy snap for a princely sum. No thanks.

I was wet. I was cold. I was starving. Thankfully I'd brought my own food as the food on location was also being sold at extortionate tourist rates. Such a shame really. I left hoping that John O'Groats did not follow suit with its counterpart at the other end.

I understand that there are more tourists down south and therefore potentially more upkeep costs, but I don't think this was the way to do it.

Anyways, we took our own happy snaps nearish to the sign, ate our sandwiches under the shelter of the tacky tourist memorabilia arcade and then I headed back out into the rain to run back to where we'd left the van.

That hill I mentioned that had the cyclists walking up … yeah it was still there and like those riders from earlier in the day, it was a slow trudge up to the top for me too. I told Sharif about my Puffing Billy mantra that I would share with all the people I'd trained over the years to run up hills. Puffing Billy was an Australian TV train character from my youth. When he had a heavy load or a big hill to climb, he'd say to himself 'I … think … I … can … I … think … I … can', which would get faster as he built up momentum 'I think I can, I think I can, I think I can'. Back when I was coaching, I would get my running team to look up to the top of the hill and say 'I think I can, I know I can' and then set them onwards and upwards. As they ran up and it got tougher, I'd be next to them urging them to say the mantra over and over and over again 'I know I can, I know I can'.

Today had been the end of week six. It had been wet and windy, it had killer hills, my back had become soaked from the excessive rain and was now red raw and blistered from my backpack, but I kept on repeating to myself 'I know I can, I know I can'.

The strength of belief
Is from never giving up
'I can' becomes fact

~ Nikki Love

WEEK 7

DAY 43. EXMOUTH & DAWLISH, DEVON

Sunday 8th October, 2017

Daily distance: 42.7km

Time taken: 6hrs 42mins

Total adventure distance: 1842.4km

Don't you just love English weather ... just as quickly as the foul weather had blown in, it blew out and we woke to stunning blue skies for today's run from Exmouth to Dawlish and back along the Exmouth Trail.

With the sun shining, I set off in a jolly mood. We were on the calm side of the UK coastline and as I ran, I watched the waves rhythmically roll in and ebb out. It was mesmerising, it was as if they were calling out to me, 'Hey Nic, come and play'. It was my turn to say, 'Let's come back here when this stooopid adventure is done'. Sharif nodded and rode on slightly ahead, making sure that I kept the momentum moving forward, and did not get side-tracked into playing in the water. We were moving into week seven – only three more weeks of effort and then we'd have all the time in the world to play on a sandy shore.

Iggy Rassool and Richard Thompson were clients from my previous life back in Leicester as a sports therapist and coach. They were in the area doing a beer brewing course for the weekend and they'd thought that a run would be a great way to get over a hangover from their previous night's drinking – their idea, not mine, I should point out. They joined us shortly after my halfway point.

Having company was a great distraction from the tiredness that I was feeling, and with other people to keep me talking and running, it turns out that it also provided some stress relief for Sharif.

Let me share another insight into ultra-running over multiple weeks, not only is it not a glamorous sport, but it's also a bit self-ish. I was focussed on me and keeping me going, and although I was aware of Sharif, I was not really taking notice of his struggles.

Being the support crew is tough, not only was he making sure that I got through my day, he also had to think about where we were going to stay, how we were going to eat, where we were going to run, who was going to meet us and where. The original plan that I'd put together, had long been thrown out the window and main-taining fluidity with some form of direction and coordination was down to Sharif.

He was my project manager, driver, income provider, cook, cof-fee fairy, and far too often my wailing wall. He was also my love, and he had to watch the person that he loved struggle with pain, tiredness, emotional and hormonal roller-coasters (genuinely, peri-menopause is the pits), hot flushes that were interrupting my sleep and in turn, his. It was hard and he had no-one to lean on because I was so wrapped up in my own focus of 'keep on going'.

As it was a warm day, and I'd been running well with Iggy and Richard pushing me along, and as I was well into the second half of my day, we thought we'd introduce the guys to my new mara-thon tactic of a mid-marathon beer. As I mentioned, I'd coached both of these guys and this was a little different to my usual eat healthy, train conscientiously, 'your body is a temple' message that I had preached way back before I'd taken on this crazy adventure. I'd changed and I was inviting them to embrace the change with me.

It was a glorious Sunday afternoon, the beer garden was full to overflowing, and although we looked a little out of place having a pint in our sweaty running kit, we did notice a big group sitting on the grass, with bicycles by their sides, tucking into bottles of rosé.

As we got back on the trail, Sharif and I had a chat with Iggy and Richard about what we wanted to do when this was all over and the suggestion of cycling to the pub, having a drink or three then cycling home was put on the table – yes that would be a lovely way to spend a Sunday afternoon, what could go wrong with that?

I still had a distance to go when we said goodbye to the fellas, they had to hoof it back to Leicester, and as I trundled along feeling a little bit meh and sorry for myself we heard and then saw the group of cyclists we'd seen at our pub stop coming along the path.

We watched on as they weaved, giggled and ultimately crashed.

Thankfully, they were in fits of laughter when we rushed over to help. They were okay, mainly embarrassed. They got back up, dusted themselves off and rode off into the sunset. I hoped they hadn't got too far to travel, they'd fallen awfully close to the river bank – ah, perhaps riding to our favourite watering hole, drinking the afternoon away and then riding home was not that great of an idea after all.

Instead of a night in the van, we opted for a night in a hotel despite our budget saying it was not really feasible to stay in a hotel. I needed a shower, I needed a good bed, and as we sat in the hotel restaurant waiting for our food, the tears came.

During the first week, my back had suffered with chaffing, rubbing and blistering from my backpack but with a lot of Vaseline and the use of tea tree oil in the evenings, my skin had repaired and toughened up to the task at hand. However, during yesterday's run to Land's End, I'd got so wet that my back had blistered again and today I'd made the original rookie mistake and not applied Vaseline to my already red and raw back.

I was so tired, and it was so emotionally draining to keep going, but this was what I'd signed up to do, and even though it hurt, I was going to keep going because I knew I'd feel different in the morning.

I also knew that one day I probably wouldn't be able to do this - today was not going to be that day.

DAY 44. SYDLING ST NICHOLAS, DORSET

Monday 9th October, 2017

Daily distance: 42.5km

Time taken: 7hrs 3mins

Total adventure distance: 1884.9km

When I chose my original sixty-three locations, the criteria I had used was that I was looking for iconic UK landmarks and then checking to see if an ultra or marathon course already existed at that location.

Sydling St Nicholas was one of the locations I'd earmarked, but as Sharif and I looked at the maps for a route, we couldn't find anything of notable interest – running or otherwise.

Maybe I'd chosen it as simply a good stopping off point between yesterday's and tomorrow's marathon locations. We were putting in some long-distance post marathon drives so I think this location had been a compromise.

For whatever reasons, it was an idyllic English countryside location with nice, quiet country lanes to knock out another 42.2kms. We parked up at the village pub the Greyhound Inn (with their permission), I slathered my back in Vaseline and off I trotted down the country lane with Sharif on Scotty the Bike.

I don't think I've ever seen so many pheasants in all of my life. The fields were covered in them. They are such funny birds. They're very skittish, they make weird, high-pitched squealing noises when they are disturbed and when they fly you can hear their wings cutting through the air. For such a pretty bird, they really are not very graceful and perhaps because of their skittishness they come across as quite a silly bird too – if they are close to a fence they will try and escape by running repeatedly into the fence until they realise they've got wings and that they can go up and over it.

This marathon came and went without too much of a hitch. I was tired, so we kept it nice and flat. There were a few opportunities to take some trail paths, but they soon started heading upwards, so I retreated back down and kept to the roads.

Today's pheasant watching run was much like my recovery marathon run at home - quiet, pretty to look at, easy to run and gather myself, and a lovely pub to finish in at the end.

Can't complain about that.

DAY 45. BRIGHTON & HOVE, EAST SUSSEX

Tuesday 10th October, 2017

Daily distance: 42.7km

Time taken: 6hrs 57mins

Total adventure distance: 1927.6km

I'd run the Brighton marathon back in 2011, posting my fastest marathon time to date, and done on a minimal amount of long-distance training.

At that point in my life I was testing myself to see whether I could do only body strength workouts and run short distances 5-10kms, yet still pull off an occasional long distance run – by occasional I mean that I ran one marathon in 2011.

It appeared that I could, although the second half of that 2011 marathon was completed through sheer grit and determination to not give up and get to the finish line. At the time, I didn't know that one day I was going to do 63 marathons and that I would be relying so heavily on the 'grit and determination' tactic, but I am proof that minimal distance training can work.

My thoughts went back to 2011. It was a bright, sunny and relatively windless day, although as a coastal town there always tends to be some wind. The marathon course winds its way through the city and out and back along the coastline. I recalled that it was a little undulating at the halfway turn, but I remembered it fondly.

This day in 2017, the wind was up, and it was drizzly, but the sun did come out in bursts. The wind was fantastic when it was a tail wind, but it was only a tailwind in one direction which was the way out of Brighton. We were staying in Brighton, so at some point I had to turn back and face the wind.

The strong wind did lead to some fierce waves hitting the wall along the foreshore which lead to one of my favourite photos of me running along and getting hit by the spray of a wave. Full disclosure, it took about three or four attempts of me running past the wall to capture the moment the wave spray hit perfectly over my head, but all that distance counted towards my total marathon distance, so it was nice to have a bit of fun as well as run.

The headwind along the foreshore was fierce, and as I battled along, I joined stride with a gent, Keith Patmore, who was pushing through the wind at my pace. In sync, we started to chat about the Brighton marathon, about running in general and the benefits it brings to our lives. I enjoyed remembering just how much running had brought to my life, and it was lovely hearing Keith's view on what it had brought to his. We concluded that it's not always about running for times or distances, it's often about being in the beauty of nature, about taking time out to breath and to calm the mind, it's about connecting to your body knowing that you are looking after it, giving it love and respect.

It also provides lovely opportunities to meet new friends, and I thoroughly enjoyed my time with Keith. However, he was out for a bit of a jog, and I was out to complete a marathon, so I had to say goodbye to him and continue on my own. Well, I say on my own, Sharif was still riding along by my side but we'd got into a routine whereby he'd ride near me but give me quiet time and thinking space until he'd notice me dipping. There was a tipping point for me as the day drew on and I got more tired, my brain would sometimes wander off into some dark places that were tough to get out of.

As I struggled into the headwind, I started questioning why I was doing this. I knew it was tiredness, but I was struggling watching so many people jog on by me like they were out on a Sunday stroll.

Sharif was getting to be a dab hand at reading my moods and he knew when he needed to step in. He pointed out, that those people running on by me hadn't done 44 marathons in the previous 44 days, so chances are they were feeling fresh. But I was on a downward spiral. The more I shuffled and watched others run by me, the more I questioned my ability to run, and the more I started letting negative thoughts get into my head. What were they thinking of me as they passed? What were people going to say about me when they looked at each of my marathon times?

I stopped to get some food inside me, I was drained. And then the tears started. Before I knew it, I was sitting on the ground saying I couldn't go on anymore. This was just way too hard. I was not a good enough runner to finish it. It was too much.

Sharif watched on as I had my teary half-tantrum – I truly didn't have the energy to get into full-tantrum mode. He gave me a cuddle as the tears streamed down my face and I ate my sandwiches.

I'd spent hours talking to Sharif before we had started this adventure about all the potential scenarios I'd have to face. Being so tired that I'd consider giving up was one of them. Sharif had spent so many days and nights listening to me explain why I wanted to do this adventure. Why it was so important to me. The charity reasons, my friendship with Dirk reasons, my personal reasons of wanting to prove to myself that I could see this through to the end. He knew what to do.

He sat calmy beside me and repeated back all my whys. Getting me to join in the conversation as my tears stopped flowing.

I said, 'It hurts.' He replied, 'Yes, but you knew it would.'

I said, 'I'm tired.' He replied, 'Yes, but you knew you would be.'

He then asked, 'Are you truly done?'.

The answer was no.

I stood up and he said, 'Just keep putting one foot in front of the other and remember why.'

My whys flooded back into my mind. My dreams and thoughts and reasons that I'd written in my journal about and trained with for so many years all came flooding back.

My fight came back. My feet started moving.

'I know I can, I know I can' – my chant was back.

I shuffled on, into the cold head wind that was still there doing its best to pound me into submission, but that was not going to happen, not today! I was going to pound right back, step by step, minute by minute, hour by hour until I hit my magic number 42.2kms. I had made a commitment – to myself, to the charity, to my friends and family. I would not give up, I would not give in.

Onwards …

We were so very appreciative to have the support of the Hilton Hotels during this adventure and that night we had been gifted a beautiful room in the Brighton Hilton Metropole, which was situated front and centre on the foreshore.

It was grand and posh, and it had revolving doors.

My eyes lit up.

I'd got through today and now it was time for some fun – after all love, fun and adventure were the three criteria I wanted to live my life by, and if I couldn't relate what I was doing to these three filters then what was the point?

At 5:35pm two very smelly and very bedraggled people larked about on the revolving doors, on the posh furniture, somehow finding the energy to run up, down and side-shuffle with jazz hands, across the grand staircase, capturing photos and videos for when they became old and grey and 63 for reals and probably wouldn't be able to remember just what they'd managed to achieve during their end-of-summer, stooopid, crazy-assed adventure of 2017. They went 'live' on Facebook so that everyone following the daily drama of 'will she or won't she run 63 marathons in 63 days' knew that she had survived to play another day.

Our room had fresh fruit and a note saying congratulations and good luck for the rest of my challenge. It was a grand hotel and I truly felt like a queen, although I perhaps didn't look or behave quite like a queen – unless of course you can picture a rather ravenous queen in grubby tracky-daks who shovels a burger, fries and beer into her mouth with her fingers like she's never been fed before, but that's just the way I roll.

This marathon had been tough, I had gone into some quite dark places of self-doubt and self-criticism, but I also experienced self-love, self-appreciation.

It's a funny old thing running a marathon – it really gives you time to experience so many emotions and at the end, with time to reflect, I believe that I always finish my days as a better, more understanding person.

Don't get me wrong, I went on to have many more tough days when all the doubts and fears came flooding back, but I also knew from all the actual experiences that I would get through them.

DAY 46. BRIGHTON TO CRAWLEY, EAST SUSSEX

Wednesday 11th October, 2017

Daily distance: 43.7km

Time taken: 7hrs 13mins

Total adventure distance: 1971.3km

A marathon is a marathon is a marathon. It doesn't matter how fast or slow you do it, you will still need to complete 42.195kms for it to be a marathon. According to my iPhone, I take approximately 60,000 steps to complete 42.195kms. However, the marathon distance feels different when you are running it linear from one point to another even though I know it's not.

Today's marathon was just that, linear from Brighton to Crawley, and I was hoping that the wind direction hadn't changed from yesterday as it would mean I'd have a tailwind pretty much most of the way.

It hadn't (changed).

I did (have a tailwind).

And I bounced back from the funk I'd been in at the end of yesterday's marathon.

There's a cycle path from Brighton to London which was my route for the day, although I wasn't quite heading to London, I was cutting off to visit the Hollingsworth family who had been following me on Facebook and had kindly offered us a bed and a washing machine. I did warn them that my kit was stinky, and their machine may never be the same again – hand washing in a hotel bath doesn't quite do the same job as a washing machine.

Sharif had driven ahead to the town of Crawley and was cycling back to join me with a backpack full of food. He knew that there were quite a few hills to come in the second half of my day and he wanted to make sure that I was eating enough without me having to carry all the food in my backpack. I think his tactics were that I couldn't complain with a mouthful of food.

Although I was no longer targeting all of the UK's most iconic locations for my marathons, I was still undertaking an Aussie's running-sightseeing-holiday-adventure of the UK and I don't think I was ever disappointed with the places that I did run through. The UK is full of beautiful countryside, villages, prettiness – even the odd industrial estate had its purpose and its place in the landscape.

If I did have a complaint and grump about the locations, it was seeing the amount of littering and fly-tipping that occurred. I don't understand the mentality of throwing your personal rubbish out the window of a travelling car and into nature and I don't understand the mentality of fly-tipping when there are plenty of official council tips around. I know our system of rubbish collection, recycling and disposing of our waste is not perfect, but it doesn't warrant throwing your rubbish into nature with disregard and lack of concern.

Today's rant.

DAY 47. FOLKESTONE, KENT

Thursday 12th October, 2017

Daily distance: 42.5km

Time taken: 7hrs 27mins

Total adventure distance: 2013.8km

I'd been looking forward to this day for many weeks now. Today I was meeting in person and running with my new cyber buddy Andy Vandenberg.

Social media has a lot of knockers and I understand why, it can be quite overwhelming, intimidating and sometimes a bit nasty. Trolls have become a real thing, not just those nasty fairy-tale characters. The ability to write nasty, hurtful, negative comments from the comfort of home, behind a screen, not looking face to face with a person is sadly real. On the other hand, social media can bring people from all around the world a little closer and there is the opportunity to chat and laugh and even meet with people from outside our immediate physical neighbourhood. I'd been recommended to follow this guy with the Instagram name 'chubstomarathon' – an Aussie guy living in the UK who loved to push himself and share how he was getting on with this thing called life, and today we would be running together for reals.

Folkestone was his 6th marathon in a row and my 47th. Needless to say, we were both feeling the strains of doing something way out of our comfort zones which gave us quite a lot to talk about that day. Andy had another running friend, Hannah Beam, joining us for the whole day and Sharif was going to cycle some and run the last half with us.

As we ran, we exchanged the highs, the lows and our tummy grumbles. We laughed, ate ice-cream, played on swings and slides in the kiddies' playground - I don't ever want to feel like I'm too old to play like a kid.

We ran strong for some. We walked for some. We did that something in between - a run/walk shuffle, and there were a few tears — this stuff hurts.

Andy and I both agreed that the route along the Folkestone promenade, where the waves rolled in and hit the stones and shells of the shoreline, was pretty enough but it wasn't anywhere near as nice as any Aussie beach. That's where our friendly agreement ended, and our friendly heated debate began — Which Australian beach was in fact the best beach in the world?

We are from two different states of Australia, so we were always going to be a little biased by our own home-town beaches, but as this is my book and not his, I can confirm that any of the surf beaches in my home state of Victoria could be crowned the best beach in the world — Torquay, Jan Juc, Winkypop, Bell's Beach, the list was endless. Sorry Andy, you lose!

Apart from our friendly best-beach-banter, today had been a bit of a party atmosphere compared to the previous few days of spending a lot of time on my own. It had kept my head clear of the negative dips, although there were still some tears.

We shared tears of pain and tiredness throughout the day, but we also shared tears of amazement and love when we finished, I like those kinds of tears.

Each day was bringing so many emotions and I thought that it was my tiredness that seemed to be overexaggerating everything.

It may have been for the most part, but there was another thing at play with me, and it wasn't until I looked back retrospectively and learned more about peri-menopausal symptoms - heightened anxiety, extreme fatigue, hormonal mood swings, hot flushes, changes in menstrual flow - that I realised I was trying to take on a challenge that was extremely hard on my body whilst dealing with this phase of my life which is also hard on a woman's body.

I had my period three times during my 63 days and in the days before my blood flow (these past couple of days), the peri-meno-pause symptoms would hit new heights of extremes, especially through the evenings when I would cry at the drop of a hat and my fears and doubts would be screaming in my head, which inev-itably came out in negative sentences through the night. My sleep suffered, and I needed a lot of sleep to get over the day and set myself up for the next day. I felt like I was running on empty not just in my legs but in my positivity to be able to complete this adventure.

DAY 48. LONDON, LONDON

Friday 13th October, 2017

Daily distance: 43.0km

Time taken: 6hrs 34mins

Total adventure distance: 2056.8 km

We were given the luxury of another complimentary night's stay in another lovely Hilton Hotel which was very timely.

We had a long drive from Folkestone to London, I was knackered, and I really appreciated having toilet facilities and a comfortable bed. As I showered Sharif headed out and brought back burgers, fries and a beer - as well as a lovely place to stay I needed calories, calories, and more calories.

Today we were taking in all the iconic sights of London, starting from our hotel which whilst not iconic, was perfectly located just a short jog away from the banks of the River Thames which were full to bursting with iconic London places and things to see.

Debbie Hollingsworth had travelled from Crawley and was waiting patiently a few kilometres along the river, we may have misjudged just how long it took for my legs to warm up to today's marathon, but she didn't mind, she was happy, she was having a day off and a pootle around Ol' Lahndon Town (which is the way you're supposed to say it if you're a Londoner ... maybe).

I was having a strange day. I know I probably hadn't eaten enough the night before, but my head was really struggling to get into the game, and I was struggling to remember words.

Feeling vague, or brain foggy, is yet another peri-menopausal symptom which I was unaware of at the time and a new experience in this adventure, but in retrospect it explained what I was experiencing.

I found it hard to get into a rhythm, I was hungry, hormonal and there were a lot more people that I had to dodge - Friday along the Thames is a busy time. The upside, however, of being at day 48 of this adventure, was that I knew if I just kept going that I'd get through this weird day.

Another friend, Anne Iarchy, joined our little running posse a bit later in the day and although I was struggling to find my running groove, I really appreciated having people around. We ran and selfie'd our way around London grabbing happy snaps at Tower Bridge, Westminster, Big Ben, Buckingham Palace until the girls had to head home, leaving me and Sharif to shuffle around Hyde Park to finish the day.

Shuffling along the pathway, a man ahead in the distance with a flat cap was waving us down. Sharif had organised a little surprise for the end of the day, Simon – you remember Simon from day one, John O'Groats – well Simon was in London for work and throughout the day, he'd been in contact with Sharif to coordinate where he could catch us up. He found us just as I shuffled my last few metres of marathon 48, and he'd brought some of his John O'Groats Golden pale ale too, what a superstar!

I was keen to find out how he'd got on after his herculean effort to run a marathon having not run any further than 10km prior. He said that he proudly limped about the entire following week and continuously told his mates all about how he had completed it, when they all thought he couldn't. I was so pleased for him that he'd earned those bragging rights.

He mentioned that he had no concept of how I'd managed to get up and run the next day let alone the weeks that followed. At this point, I was starting to wonder how I was going to get up the next day too. I felt completely spent and I had yet another little cry as I waved Simon off into his cab for his long train trip back home to Scotland. It was only then that I realised that we hadn't finished where we'd started this morning and that we were going to have to walk back to the hotel.

It wasn't a huge long walk, but I knew I wasn't going to walk it on an empty stomach so we headed out of the park to the bustling side streets of Kensington, found a pub and settled in for a very much needed meal. Thankfully, it was a pub that believed in ma-hooosive servings too.

With my legs rested a bit, a lot of very highly calorific and very delicious food in my belly, and a catch up on social media to read all the lovely words of encouragement and support, I was able to pick myself up and stroll on back to the hotel.

I may have struggled today, but I knew that I'd be able to get up and go the next day, my whys were too important to me not to.

DAY 49. BUSHY PARK, LONDON

Saturday 14th October, 2017

Daily distance: 42.3km

Time taken: 7hrs 3mins

Total adventure distance: 2099.1km

As it was a Saturday, and as we were pretty darn close to the home of the first official Parkrun, my first 5kms was going to be the Bushy Park Parkrun.

Making my way over to the start line a man came up to me and asked if I was Nikki. Yep, that's me. He said, 'I thought I recognised you, I've been following your adventure. I just want to say thank you for what you're doing for HDA.'

Simon Maples introduced himself and went on to tell me his story and how this horrible disease was impacting his family.

Oh my, the tears flowed, but this was one of the big reasons why I was willing to push myself beyond the tiredness, the aches and the doubts. I knew that what I was doing was nothing compared to what the families and the people who have Huntington's have to put up with day in, day out, forever. My challenge was only nine weeks long, I could do this for nine weeks.

These were the conversations I was having out loud and in my head, but as my day wore on, I still hit that point where I didn't think there was much more left of me to give to cover the final few miles.

Having a dodgy belly that required me to find jungle looking bushes to hide behind had become quite the norm for me and whilst I was running in the English countryside along quiet lanes and paths, being able to dash behind bushes was relatively easy. Running in cities and city parks was a little trickier, there was limited 'jungle' looking quiet places to dash to and there were people everywhere.

As well as meeting Simon for the Parkrun section of the day, another friend, Colette Mason, had turned up with her bike and together with Sharif, they became my bike brigade. Their job for the day was to tag team me, one stayed with me urging me to hold on just a little longer, whilst the other rode off to find the next public toilet for me to get to. A fun game.

Bushy Park is the second largest of London's Royal Parks and is home to approximately 320 deer, of which I believe 100 or so are stags. It was rutting and mating season and throughout the day we watched on as the single stags, hoping to commandeer some of the female deer, strutted their stuff whilst the stag daddy bellowed loudly warning them to stay away from his harem.

My head was a little light and without thinking it through I started heading towards a stag to get a better picture. I really was in no condition to outrun a stag if it decided to charge me and yet there I was saying 'Hey little stag, come here little stag'. Thankfully, Colette was there to call me back to safety 'Hey little Nikki, come here little Nikki'. I was losing the plot.

Simon and his family were waiting for me at the carpark for my finish. There was an added incentive of an ice-cream van waiting too, so I shuffled on as best I could to get to the last little bit. Oh, those last little bits were a killer, why did I not do the 0.2kms at the start of my run when I'm feeling fresh instead of at the end after 42 kilometres?

With ice-cream in my belly and the loud cheers of Colette, Sharif, Simon and his family, I circled around and around the car park until all my GPS gear ticked over the 42.2kms.

Day done, Sharif bundled me into my Dryrobe, big hugs and more tears were given out as I said goodbye to the wonderful team I'd had for the day. Colette pointed us in the direction of the best fish and chip shop in town, we needed a lot of sustenance and I personally needed to restock my belly – today's marathon had been extra hard on it. Finally, it was time to rest.

Well kind of, Sharif had a three-hour drive ahead to get us to the HDA's Annual Conference, which was being held at the Raddison Blu Hotel, Leicester.

What's success to you?
Time or place does not define,
heart and effort does.

~ Nikki Love

WEEK 8

DAY 50. LEICESTER MARATHON, LEICESTERSHIRE

Sunday 15th October, 2017

Daily distance: 43.7km

Time taken: 6hrs 12mins

Total adventure distance: 2142.8km

Marathon 50 was to be my second official marathon race and it was in my other hometown, Leicester. I was looking forward to catching up with so many friends and clients and running locations that had been the base of my training and ambitions ... I nearly didn't get there.

Turns out, running 49 marathons in a row does not bode well for being able to party into the wee small hours.

We'd been invited to attend the HDA Annual Conference, which after a certain time in the proceedings became a fancy-dress party. Arriving quite late we made a brief appearance – I went dressed as an ultra-runner who was knackered after completing 49 marathons in a row and Sharif went as my driver – we didn't stay long.

Thankfully one of my long-time friends, and one of Dirk's best mates, Danny Keane, is the General Manager of the Radisson Blu Hotel and he'd provided us with a beautiful complimentary room to rest our weary heads ... We were not the problem.

I'm not sure what happened through the night with Stan the Van. Maybe he snuck into the fancy dress party after we had gone to bed, perhaps dressed as a van that worked, and partied the night away. All we knew was that when we needed to head off to the start of marathon 50, he decided to have a hissy fit and refused to start. Thankfully, the hotel's coach driver was able to come to our rescue and get old Stan on the move.

We eventually high-tailed it into the centre of Leicester, and as is the case with city races, the roads around the start and throughout the city were closed. Sharif got the van as close as he could, I then hoofed it across parks and fields for what felt like the longest distance ever.

Honestly – running fast, before running a marathon, after running 49 previous marathons – what a ridiculous start to a day (it was probably less than a kilometre, but I do like to be a bit of drama queen).

I made it just in time for the starting gun and turns out I needed every minute of my marathon run to count. My marathons were taking anything between six and half to eight and a half hours to complete. Granted, the longer ones were often due to me visiting schools, giving talks, or taking an excessive number of selfies.

Apparently, there was a cut off time of 6 hours and 15 minutes for today's marathon – a little piece of information that was shared with me during the marathon.

The half marathoners and the full marathoners run together through the city of Leicester up to mile 6 then they part ways.

I was happily trundling along with other runners around me only to discover when we split at that mile 6 point that there were no runners around me or behind me. I was the last of the full distance runners and from then on, I had the company of the sweeper car cruising behind me, who informed me of the cut off time.

It was their job to make sure the last of the runners (me) were doing okay and as they travelled along, the roads behind would re-open. They kept me advised as to how much wriggle room I had between my pace and the cut off pace and as the day wore on, the closer I dropped to that bugger of a cut-off time.

My usual practice of stopping for selfies was being impinged. 'Don't stop, you're falling behind!' was yelled out to me several times as I'd attempt to grab a photo of a landmark. Incentivising or what!

I did appreciate having the sweeper car behind me, but I struggled to do my usual stop, eat, stretch, run for fear of being told I had fallen behind and was out of the race. Thankfully, I had many drop in friends on bikes who came to join me for bits which gave me more focus on chatting and less on the distance I had to run. Time and miles fly by when you're chatting.

I was heading towards the mile 17 marker when I noticed runners ahead. Woohoo, I was starting to catch up, the tortoise was coming into her own.

My new friends, the cut-off time brigade, yelled out that they would meet me at the other end of Watermead Country Park, this was not an area for cars. I was cool with that as I knew the lakes like the back of my hand.

A marathon, or 42.2 kilometres or 26.2 miles, whichever way you describe it, is a bloody long way. It plays with your head. It gets hard. Your body starts to hurt. Thoughts get louder. The questions start popping up. Can I do this? Why am I doing this? I can't do this.

For each question, the brain will quickly search for a response, example flashbacks, other thoughts associated with that thought.

It's when the word 'can't' shows up that you have to nip it in the bud. A downward spiral is fast, possibly faster than an upward one, to create.

As I started to catch up, run with and then pass people, I either had a little chat or gave as many encouraging words as I could. I'd been in this place of a marathon many, many times. I knew how they were feeling, and I knew what I liked to hear.

'Keep your head in the game.'

'Remember the reason why you're here, even if it now seems to be the dumbest reason in the whole wide-world - you thought it, and therefore it was a reason.'

That last sentence were words that I spoke to one particular woman that I ran with that day. As we ran together, she mentioned that it had been a drunken bet to take part in the marathon.

A drunken bet may have been the reason, but somewhere in her booze-fuelled mind she'd thought that maybe she was capable of doing this and so she put herself into the game. Somewhere in her thinking, she wanted to prove herself right and that was what she had to hold on to right now and keep taking those steps even when they were hurting like crazy. She wanted to prove herself right.

I wanted to prove myself right on so many levels. Today's little task was to prove to myself that I could do a marathon within the cut off time.

Sure enough, at the end of the park, the sweeper car was waiting with some news. They were finishing up for the day as us last lot of runners had fallen behind the cut off time for this section, meaning that the road closures ahead were about to open and the remaining aid stations would be closed ... we could keep going if we wanted.

Oh man, that news sucked.

I wasn't exactly sure of the route from that point on, but they said it should still be marked. I was a bit worried 'should' sounded flaky. I'm not the best at navigating, but I figured even if I took a wrong turn and went off-piste, I knew roughly the direction to take and I'd eventually get to the finish line. I'd simply keep running until I hit the full marathon distance.

Luckily a few volunteers heard the news and said they'd stick with me on their bike and make sure I didn't get lost. As it turned out, I had people waiting ahead to join me. Sharif turned up on his bike. Sarah Bulfield, having already run her half marathon had made her way back to mile 23 and was waiting to run me through to the finish.

Riley and Charlotte, Sharif's youngest daughter, were also waiting in the last kilometre to join me. They were in their civilian kit and were pretty much walking to my running pace and making fun of this fact, but it was so nice to have them along with me.

I headed down the final stretch towards the finish line, faithful friends who had waited such a long time, cheered loud and I found my kick again.

I looked up at the clock.

I had made the cut off time 6:12!

I had proved myself right!

I can.

After two weeks on the road, we were heading back home, I could not wait, but first it was pick up Rufus time, followed by a quick celebratory beer with the kids, Willis, Sharif and me at the pub where I had originally met Sharif.

We had a little laugh together about how that coffee date had led to all of this.

DAYS 51-53. RECOVERY MARATHON, NOTTINGHAMSHIRE

Monday 16th October, 2017

Daily distance: 42.5km

Time taken: 7hrs 8mins

Total adventure distance: 2184.5km

Tuesday 17th October, 2017

Daily distance: 42.9km

Time taken: 6hrs 44mins

Total adventure distance: 2228.2km

Wednesday 18th October, 2017

Daily distance: 43.3km

Time taken: 6hrs 48mins

Total adventure distance: 2271.5km

After being on the road for what felt like forever, we were back home, which meant I had some recovery marathons ahead of me. Just as well really, yesterday's speedy (for me) marathon had taken its toll and I had woken with extra empty legs and a cold sore-swollen bottom lip.

As my cold sore and I headed out on the morning of my 51st marathon, I recalled Ben Smith's advice from marathon 39 - that it would get easier after marathon 50 ... ahhhh, nope!

The sky was looking a little weird. The day went on, and the sky became more eerie. A storm was blowing in.

Storm Ophelia was heading towards the UK and with her, she was bringing sand particles from the Sahara, debris from forest fires in Portugal and Spain and the rather warmer than normal weather we'd had over the weekend.

The sky was thick with all these particles which turned the sun a deep orange/red and brought a quietness to my run ... really eerie, but I loved it!

My easy, breezy Grantham Canal, Beeston Canal and River Trent runs meant lots of flat loops via home, which was just what I needed. Despite my best efforts to eat more, my weight had dropped again during the stint on the road. Being back home gave me the opportunity to get more food into me before I left in the morning, then plenty of home returns for even more food every 12 to 15 kilometres throughout the day. And of course, my little running buddy, Rufus, was back with me which made me very happy.

When the word 'run' is mentioned around Rufus, she looks up at me with a big, broad beaming smile on her face. It's a genuine smile, I tell you – she just loves to run. She'll sit pretty, giving me that smile, and watch patiently as I put on my socks and shoes. Then as I rise to go, she goes nuts, running in circles around the lounge as I head towards the door.

During my recovery marathons I alternated loops with her, but she was always on that first loop with me, there was no way I could get out the door without her.

I also had the company of Karen Parkin for much of my day 53, which was definitely a highlight during these monotonous, but essential, filler days. Karen is very much like me – set us free to run at an easy, steady pace and we'll run like that all day. And that's exactly how we took the day, easy and steady.

Days 51, 52 and 53 definitely felt very *Groundhog Day*'ish, but I knew I could not get to marathon 63 without running 51 to 62.

I just had to get them done.

DAY 54. BRAMCOTE & BEESTON, NOTTINGHAMSHIRE

Thursday 19th October, 2017

Daily distance: 42.4km

Time taken: 9hrs 36mins

Total adventure distance: 2313.9km

Holy moly it was dark outside, and whilst I know I'm not a morning person and I do like to sleep in, I'm pretty sure I hadn't slept in and missed the whole of the day, yet it felt like it. The sun was well and truly hidden behind a wall to wall sky of dark and very full rain clouds.

Today was going to be a wet one, which I was not looking forward to, but silver linings and all that. The first part of my run was to get to Nottingham train station and collect my kiddo, Riley, who was bringing his bike to spend the day by my side as I shuffled my way to a couple more primary schools, Bramcote and Beeston.

I guess I'd been lucky that I hadn't had too many totally rainy days, but today was definitely making up for it and to make it more fun, my morning dodgy belly was back.

The first 10kms of my runs were involving me running and visiting all the public toilets of Nottingham. I knew where all the supermarkets, pubs, sports clubs and stores with public conveniences were along my recovery runs.

As we travelled along the Beeston canal, Riley was getting a feel of how my days panned out. I'd feel great then I'd need the loo, then it was a mad dash to get to a toilet. On repeat.

After yet another frantic dash to a pub then a re-emergence into the cold rain we went under a bridge where I suggested we take a little refuge and breather, and that's when the tears came.

I was tired. My emotions were high. The cold and rain made things tougher. I cried. Just a little bit. To let it out. Riley watched as I went through my 'I can't do this. Tears. Why am I doing this. This is why I'm doing this. Pull myself back together. I can do this. C'mon Nic, get moving' phase. It took about 5 minutes, which is a rollercoaster of emotions to go through in a short period of time.

I wasn't really keen on showing this part of my day to Riley, I wanted him to see his mum as being strong and capable, but the frailty was also a part of it and I guess what he ultimately witnessed was that despite it all, I kept my commitment and kept going.

Sharif's office was along this route of my canal run, so we popped in there to say howdy, use the facilities (me), and to get kiddo some food. I thought I'd packed enough food for us both, but a teenage boy riding a bike, albeit slowly, required more fuelling than I was carrying. A bacon roll purchased from the truck vendor for kiddo, and we were ready to keep on going to the first school.

I eventually entered my cruising phase - when it all starts to come together, my tummy settles down and the kilometres start to click over quickly – which is usually a great time of day for me. Today it was not so good when I realised that I'd missed the turn off the canal many kilometres ago and now needed to back track and run quicker to get to the first school on time.

Ahhhh, Riley was about to see my tantrum phase.

Lots of swear words came out of my mouth as I berated myself for being that stupid. I called Sharif and berated him for … well there was actually nothing to berate him for. He'd planned out my route, I was the fool who hadn't followed it. But I needed to vent my anger at my silliness, so Sharif copped a mouthful. Honestly, how he put up with me during this event was incredible. He calmed me down. Told me he'd call the school and let them know that I was running late, but I'd get there. He then suggested that I pull myself together and keep moving.

Obviously I berated him for being so level-headed, comforting and organised, but he was right, (yes Sharif, you did read that) I did pull myself together, I kept going and eventually got to my first school of the day, Bramcote Primary, as the rain took a breather. Timing!

The teacher, Kerry Morris, had her students out on the fields waiting for me to join them and just like that, with a rousing greeting from the students, my morning grumbles were gone and my smile, joy and passion to share what I was doing was back.

I gave a little talk about why I was doing this 'crazy adventure'. About my love for running, despite the occasional tears. About being ambitious to dream something this big and being brave to actually do it and I finished with an invite to join me on a little jog around the school fields.

This was always the highlight of a visit, the kids would run with me wanting to tell me their stories about how fast, or how far they could go, or what their parents could do. There was no start line or finish line or place position to achieve on these runs, it was all about running together, squealing and giggling, skipping, run-dancing, frog-jump running and having a ball. I'd hear comments about how tough it was to run, and I'd respond back with 'Yeah, but it's fun isn't it?' They'd agree, catch their breath, and then shoot off again.

I had a second school to get to, which should have been fine if I'd been on time for the first one, but as it now stood, I had to hightail it to get to Beeston Primary School before the final bell.

With a few minutes to spare, I gave a very quick chat, had a quick little scootch around the school grounds and I gave out lots of high-fives and smiles to the kids. The teachers didn't mind, they thought it was a rather novel way to end their day.

It may have been the end of the school day, but it was back out on the roads for the final kilometres home for me and Riley and … the heavens opened again.

Not only did it rain, but it also poured, and it thundered, and it lightninged. Oooh Mother Nature you were playing with me today.

In the dark, sodden through, but extremely happy and proud, we eventually made it home. I was so proud of my son. It's hard riding a bike at my running pace. It was wet and cold, which I may have mentioned once or twice already, and yet my kiddo had put up with the horrible weather and my lack of speed. He wobbled on his bike a few times, even putting his foot down into dog poo, and not once did he moan or complain.

At the end he told me that he now truly appreciated how tough this adventure was for me and how proud he was of me. Oh my. More tears, but they were tears of joy.

I was one marathon closer to the end. I was overcoming everything that was being thrown at me and I was doing it with the love of my family and making new friends along the way. What more could I ask for?

Oh, I know - maybe less rain, please Mother Nature.

DAY 55. JESSE GRAY PS, NOTTINGHAMSHIRE

Friday 20ᵗʰ October, 2017

Daily distance: 42.7km

Time taken: 6hrs 51mins

Total adventure distance: 2356.6km

Yay, Mother Nature had listened, for a bit. Today was going to be a dry one, if not a little windy, and yay, it was also another school visit day. Jesse Gray Primary was very local so there was little chance of me getting lost and no excuse for being late for assembly. I wasn't.

As well as doing a school assembly and a little run around the grounds, the school had also organised a cake bake to raise some money for the charity and as I was about to leave, two students, Lilly and Annie Judge, presented me with two of the scrumpiest fairy cakes each with numbers 63 piped on top — it was the icing on the cake, so to speak, of a wonderful school visit.

After leaving Jesse Gray Primary school with a head full of smiley memories and a belly full of cake, I made my way back to the River Trent to assume my Recovery Marathon holding positions — out along the river, around Holme Pierrepont and back to home for a 15km loop. The strong wind helped me cruise down to the river, but tail winds end up being headwinds when you turn around.

What was with the wind today?

Thankfully, the Grantham canal part of my run had tall bramble bushes on one side and long reeds on the other, making the wind a little easier to deal with and my day a little easier to get through.

Which was handy as we were about to head off out on the road again for a few days to bag me my furthest east location of this adventure.

Well, that was the plan.

DAY 56. LINCOLN, LINCOLNSHIRE

Saturday 21st October, 2017

Daily distance: 43.3km

Time taken: 6hrs 56mins

Total adventure distance: 2399.9km

I had my daily running uniform:

Trainers - dry or wet, clean or muddy it didn't matter, they were going on my feet.

Socks – the same rule applied, although having been at home for the past week, it had been a delight to have clean socks to put on every day.

Shorts – I'm a shorts person, it has to be extremely, extremely cold for me to wear anything but.

Tops and backpack – I had worked out a layering system. Runderwear sports bra, long sleeve t-shirt, my Chasing extraordinary T-shirt, the charity singlet, a windproof-jacket which I thought was a rain jacket, turns out it wasn't, but it was all that I had so I used it.

Cap – it kept the sun off my face, the rain off my face and the wind outta my ears. Cold ears are a big pet-peeve of mine, which is also a reason I wear my hair in plaits, once my ears get cold, my head just doesn't work.

These were my standards, so I didn't really pay much attention to the weather news, as I knew I was going to deal with whatever was being thrown at me, but for some reason, we checked in on the news to find out what was going on with this crazy wind and rain.

Severe weather warnings, you say? Hmmm, well that explained a lot.

The eerie sandstorm and the following day of rain that I'd run through during marathons 53 and 54 were due to a storm named Ophelia and another storm by the name of Brian was going to be hitting the UK this weekend, just in time for my furthest east run in Great Yarmouth on Sunday.

First things first though, I had Saturday to contend with.

To break the travel distance up, marathon 56 was planned for Lincoln, and as it was a Saturday our start was the Lincoln Parkrun. Turns out I knew this Parkrun very well, I'd started and finished marathon 19 running loops at Boultham Park which I soon found out was the route for the Lincoln Parkrun - three and a bit loops of the park. Loops are a little boring, but it was nothing I couldn't handle, by now I'd done my fair share of running loops around car parks, I could handle loops around a pretty park.

What I struggled to handle throughout the day was the wind - it was blowing a hooley.

Out of the protection of the greenery of Boultham Park I was getting battered and the longer I ran for, the more we questioned the sanity of our plan to drive yet further east at the end of the day. Not only would we be camping in Stan through the evening, but I'd also then have to face a battering the next day along an open coastline.

Lincoln sure was a pretty run, and I'm glad I got to run it again with Sharif tagging along on the bike.

I had taken some happy snaps during marathon 19, but as I was running with somebody, I didn't spend too much time hanging around and reading the plaques and info scattered around the historic city's streets. This time I did. Did you know that the Lincoln cathedral was built in 1311, and once boasted that it was the tallest building in the world?

Quite by luck, the first time I had run this route, I ran down the only doozy of a hill in the county. Quite by plan, on this second visit to Lincoln, I took Sharif down the wonderfully steep and very cobbled hill. He agreed, it was a doozy.

Back at the van, we had to make a decision. Go on or go home.

I'd been battered by the wind today and the severe weather warnings were for worse tomorrow and as much as I had wanted to say that I'd run at the furthest north, south, west and east points of mainland UK, being safe and feeling strong for my final week was more important to me, I chose home.

It was a long drive home as Brian battered Old Stan all the way – I think it had been a good choice.

Dare to dream your life.
Take action, create your real,
Wear with love, truth, pride!

~ Nikki Love

WEEK 9

DAY 57. GRANTHAM CANAL, NOTTINGHAMSHIRE

Sunday 22ⁿᵈ October, 2017

Daily distance: 42.3km

Time taken: 6hrs 36mins

Total adventure distance: 2442.2km

It was wet, wild and windy outside, but I was thankful that I was at home, and running my recovery marathon route, and grateful ... I was heading into my final week!

The plan was simple, run out and back along the Grantham canal, which gave me a little bit of protection from the buffeting of Storm Brian, and repeat my loops over and over until the day was done.

I had intended on running marathon 57 at the farthest easterly point of the UK today. Instead my friends, Arwen and Phil Makin and Neil Byford, as well as my loves Sharif and Rufus, had rallied around at short notice to spend the day shuffling up and down the Grantham canal with me.

This recovery marathon route had become the route that I could run practically with my eyes closed (which, during my wake up loop, often felt exactly the way I was running – with my eyes closed).

It was a pretty simple path to run along, the canal was on one side and hedgerow on the other, all except at one place. As part of each loop, just one kilometre from my home, I had to cross the

A46, which was quite a busy loop road that skirts around Nottingham. Crossing this dual A-road involved me climbing over traffic barriers to get to a centre island, then more barriers to get to the other side. On a Grantham canal day, I would cross this road between six to eight times depending on the distance of my loops.

As my team scootched over the barriers and across the road on the first loop, Arwen asked whether I had considered taking the pedestrian crossing which was several hundred metres down the road and around a slight bend.

I had been blissfully unaware of the pedestrian crossing down the road and around the slight bend. Good to know. However, as I had successfully managed to play a human game of Frogger each and every time I'd crossed this road up until now, I decided to stick with what I'd been practicing.

I also pointed out that the traffic barriers provided wonderful resting points each and every time I crossed. I was happy to cop a squat and wait until the road was free of traffic and I was confident I was not going to become a squashed frog.

'Onwards Nikki,' I kept repeating, 'Onwards'.

DAY 58. GRANTHAM CANAL, NOTTINGHAMSHIRE

Monday 23rd October, 2017

Daily distance: 42.5km

Time taken: 7hrs 37mins

Total adventure distance: 2484.7km

I woke with the thought – I was 'ruly and truly' going to do this thing that had been inside my head for nearly seven years. I now had less than seven days to get through. Amazing!

These first two days of my final week were all about getting them done and setting the scene for the final blast which involved more primary school visits, a pub-crawl marathon – yes plans were afoot for a party marathon, and then the final day.

To help me get through today, Rufus and one of my original 7in7 crew, Amanda Lloyd, and all the people on Facebook Live kept me company along my wake-up loop of Grantham canal. This also included a brief catch up with Canal Peter – he doesn't walk Diesel the dog on a Sunday, so I'd missed him yesterday. Peter gave me his run down on what had been occurring along the canal and wished me luck for my finish, as this was probably the last time I'd see him until I really was doing a recovery run after the 63 marathons – which was definitely not going to be a marathon – along the Grantham canal.

Debbie Crouch and Clare Biddel kept me company on the Holme Pierrepont loop of my day making sure I kept a strong and steady pace. And finally, Rufus and Sharif joined me ensuring that those final bits were done and dusted.

DAY 59. CHARNWOOD SCHOOLS, LEICESTERSHIRE

Tuesday 24th October, 2017

Daily distance: 43.7km

Time taken: 7hrs 1mins

Total adventure distance: 2528.4km

Back in Leicester I had two new schools to visit along my run, as well as the company of Katherine Dean for the majority of the day and my good friend El for the final hour.

Katherine had heard about me via Facebook and being a very capable marathon runner, she was keen to join me for the full marathon distance. What she hadn't anticipated was that running at my pace, meant that she was going to be on her feet for a whole lot longer than she'd ever done before. I'd had quite a few long-distance runners join me up to this point, and the going slower and taking longer had impacted them. It really is hard running slower than your normal, comfortable pace for a very long distance.

Katherine was not deterred, and she joined me for both primary school visits which provided me with external feedback about my school visits and the impact my storytelling was having. I loved being able to talk to the kids, but I genuinely wanted them to benefit and comprehend my message of what you can achieve when you set your mind to believe.

Newtown Linford was my morning school visit – a small school with one class per year level. The smaller student numbers provided an intimate school assembly and me the opportunity to talk passionately and answer lots of questions about my adventure and there were a lot of brilliant questions including who had inspired me. I shared the names of my heroes and suggested that they look up Rosie Swale Pope MBE in particular. Rosie is a genuine British icon and her name really should be known by all, especially young girls, as someone who has completed amazing adventures and has an enormous heart that is full of love and kindness.

My afternoon school visit was at Christ Church and St Peters CE Primary School where I was invited into the classroom and my teacher friend George Parkes. She too had been following my adventure. Prior to my visit, I'd asked George if she could ask her students what they thought chasing extraordinary meant to them and we'd discuss during my visit.

Again, a small classroom provided the opportunity for an in-depth Q&A session. One young chap asked, 'What do your family and friends think about your run?'

'They think I'm a bit crazy', I responded. The word 'crazy' had been used many, many times - in a good way. It was describing doing something that was beyond normal and the comprehension of most people. I was okay with crazy.

What I got back after this comment though, really struck me.

He responded back with, 'Oh no Nikki, we think you're amazing and determined and committed,' and the whole class agreed.

I took a breath.

George had asked these kids to put some thought into what chasing extraordinary means, so I asked, 'What other words could I use ... instead of crazy?'

'Persistent.'

'Resilient.'

'Brave.'

'Ambitious.'

These words were offered back. My face was ear to ear smile, with just a glint of moisture in the corner of my eyes. Ah, yes … these words were swimming around in my head.

All the students stood along the school's fence to send me off for the final bit of my day. High fiving their extended hands I squealed as much as they did.

'Good luck Nikki!', 'Run Nikki Run!' they chanted.

'Thank you, thank you, thank you!' I squealed back.

At both schools Katherine was bought to happy tears from the responses of the students – I think I was getting it right and hopefully providing a positive impact.

On my drive home I sat with the question 'How had I managed to run 59 marathons in 59 days?' and let the thoughts roll around in my head.

I genuinely was not a skilled runner in the sense of an elite Olympic marathoner. To become an elite Olympic marathon runner, the person would have to train specifically, follow a regime, eat specifically, rest specifically.

I on the other hand, came up with an idea, trained daily at the action of running without any specificity just the general idea of practice running, eating, resting, visualising that I could do this and planning the logistics.

So, if it wasn't running skills, what was it that kept me going?

DAY 60. LEICESTER SCHOOLS, LEICESTERSHIRE

Wednesday 25th October, 2017

Daily distance: 42.6km

Time taken: 6hrs 41mins

Total adventure distance: 2571km

Way back in week 3, and on day 16 of this adventure, I had promised Cas Evans, Head Teacher at Parks Primary School, that I would go back and tell the students how I had got on with my adventure.

They had been watching me, via Cas, and had taken the whole 'chasing extraordinary' concept to heart and into their classroom projects. Cas shared a video to me of her students performing the song *Believe* in front of the general public in the city centre of Leicester. Cas explained that this was their version of chasing extraordinary, they'd learned to both sing and sign the words and performed it beautifully.

And so on Day 60, as I attempted to equal the record for the most consecutive marathon distances completed by a woman, I headed back to Parks Primary School and started my day with a little chat followed by and an extremely noisy run around the school grounds chasing the extraordinary students.

Another promise I had made on that same day was to the Head Teacher of Eyres Monsell Primary, the school I had not managed to visit that day. On day 60, I had the company of Anna Harrison, a teacher from Parks and she made sure that not only did I achieve my promise to Eyres Monsell, but I also completed marathon 60.

There was a beaming smile and a little tear in my eye as I drove back home to Nottingham at the end of my day. I knew that I had three more marathons to run until I'd fully completed this adventure. But from here on in the days that I had left were, figuratively speaking, me putting the icing on a cake that had been made of hopes, dreams, beliefs, commitment, determination and resilience with a little dash of 'crazy' thrown into the baking tin to have helped the cake to rise.

DAY 61. PUB CRAWL, NOTTINGHAMSHIRE

Thursday 26th October, 2017

Daily distance: 42.9km

Time taken: 6hrs 24mins

Total adventure distance: 2613.9km

Today I was passing the target record of sixty consecutive marathon distances and it was time to get the party started so to speak. I obviously still had three entire marathons to run, but as Sharif kept telling me, I could fall the last little bit of a marathon. This was the last little bit of the entire adventure and I was going to have as much fun as you can have whilst running 42.2kms, having already run 2532kms over the prior sixty days.

The fun was that for marathon 61 we, which was Sharif, Arwen, Phil (and Rosie for the first hour), were going on a tour of Nottingham.

It was going to be a day of two halves, the first half we were visiting all the main sports grounds around Nottingham, apart from Nottingham Forest Football Club's ground, as nobody had responded to our requests - boo, Forest, boo. Anyway, I had plenty of other sports sites to see and run around.

My 'Tour of Nottingham' run commenced, and my band of merry men and women and I left my house and headed to location number one, Nottingham Rugby Club, where we were greeted by Archie, an oversized stag, the club mascot. Hands shook, happy snaps taken, and we took off for a little scootch around the grounds. We laughed and giggled our way around the pitch as

Archie struggled to run fast in his oversized shoes and I simply struggled to run fast.

Location number two, Notts County Football Club.

Notts County boasts as the oldest football club in the UK. The last time I had been at this ground, I had been there to watch Riley, as a 10-year-old, be a mini-mascot for the team as it celebrated its 150th year anniversary. The stands were full, and they cheered as Riley (with his designated football player) made his way out onto the pitch.

Today's crowd was a bit sparse, being the sum total of my team and the Director of the club. I didn't mind, I was being given a very special opportunity to walk along the runway, step out onto the pitch, and have a little run up and down the side lines.

I was thrilled with the opportunities being provided to me and was pleased that the clubs were acknowledging the scope of the challenge I was putting myself through. So, what if there were no big crowds? I had a great big imagination, which was the thing that had got me here in the first place. Sharif, Phil, Arwen and Rosie stood in the stands cheering me on – what I heard was the cheer of the crowd the day that Riley had ran out onto the pitch … and the crowd went wild.

I was thoroughly enjoying every minute of this day; it was the day I was surpassing the record and creating a new possible. Onwards to Trent Bridge Cricket Ground.

Growing up in Australia, I was brought up on cricket and I had known about Trent Bridge Cricket Ground from the infamous test match battles throughout the years between Australia and England.

Today I was getting to run down the steps from the changing rooms to the ground. I was going to have some fun with this.

At the doorway I pretended this was my cricketing debut. I stretched and limbered up at the top of the steps, I sauntered down towards the gate swinging my pretend bat. I could practically hear the crowd roar; I was definitely milking the moment.

The crowd – Sharif, Arwen, Phil and Rosie were actually mainly laughing at me, but I was having an absolute ball. It was such a thrill, and I was so looking forward to sharing the photos of this one with my cricket-loving son.

Next up was the home of Nottingham's hockey team, which is based a little way out of the city at Nottingham University campus. This obviously worked well for me, I did have 42.2 kilometres to cover, I needed to get out and about.

What a lovely surprise, the club was holding a training camp for their young, up-and-coming hockey players. I watched them knock the ball back and forth before they came over to listen to me give a little talk about following dreams. I spoke about having a dream, being brave enough to take the first step to make it come true and then the persistence and determination I had needed to get to this day, my 61st of 63. It had been tough at times, but it had been so worth the effort. I wished these kids all the best with the future that they were working on and dedicating their time to.

We headed back into the city for the last of the sporting grounds visits, the Nottingham Arena in the Lace Market district of Nottingham city centre, and home to the Nottingham Panthers Ice Hockey club.

I knew this part of the city very well. One of the many incarnations of Nikki had owned a restaurant a couple hundred of metres away from the ice stadium. Willis and I, along with several other friends, had pooled our money, our talent, and our ambition to take a risk, do something different and open a restaurant.

Was it a financial success? Nope, it was quite the opposite. You could perhaps call it a financial failure, but had it been an experience failure? Absolutely nope. We had made something from nothing. We built a team of chefs and waiting staff. We provided a classy and cool food and entertainment experience that thousands of people enjoyed.

This was at a time when personally, Willis and I had decided to separate, and we were running a business as well as navigating through a split and raising a one year old.

It was a tough time, but I know that I enhanced my own skills through it. I learned I was stronger than I thought, I could survive heartbreak, I could survive things not going right because ultimately it was up to me to define the term 'success'. I learned that it was okay to take a risk.

Today was a clear example. I'd taken many risks to create this adventure and not only was I was surviving, but I was also thriving. I was making a risky dream goal come true.

We ran past my old restaurant to the ice-stadium. I smiled. I wiped away a little tear. It was a good tear. A tear that reminded me of who I was and what I can do.

The person who was meeting and greeting us at the ice-stadium wasn't ready, 'Did we mind waiting a bit?'. I didn't mind waiting, but I couldn't just stand around, I had 42.2kms to cover. Only one thing to do, I went into one of my famous end of day car park holding patterns at the front of the Ice Stadium. I ran round and round in circles as we waited and waited for the person to come and collect us.

It was a weird but fun experience running around the stands of the empty ice-rink. I'd only ever been to one game here, many years ago. I remember the ice-puck hurtling into the crowd where we were sitting. We all ducked and covered our heads. Unfortunately, it did hit someone, the kid brother of one of our group. It brought our night to an early end as we left to make sure the young chap's brain was still intact. Ahhh, memories.

The first half of the marathon was done, the next half was going to be weird and wonderful. We were about to hit the pub-crawl phase of the day.

First pub stop, the Vat & Fiddle, which was also home of the local brewery, Castle Rock. We were meeting Graham Percy, who was going to be our host at each of the Castle Rock pubs around the city.

The Vat & Fiddle was also the workplace of one of my second cousins who was over from Australia on a bit of a gap year. Josh was in charge of pouring us all a 1/3 pint of one of Castle Rock's finest and my favourite of pale ales, the Elsie Mo. Noice.

I was having a bit of a wobble, not because of the beer, but because the car of my latest business partner was parked out the front of the pub (after closing the restaurant business, I set up a property business with someone else).

Despite being in business together, our 'working' relationship was strained and had been for many years, in a nutshell I had opted to become a silent partner of the business rather than continually clash with him. I knew that this was his favourite lunch time locale, and I hadn't been keen on stopping at this pub for this particular reason, but it was the home of the brewery. I was going to have to cope with the possibility of coming face to face with him.

We were making quite a commotion outside. Josh bringing out the beers, the camera crew wandering in and out of the pub looking for good vantage points to take photos. Most of the pub patrons that were inside came outside to see what was going on. I had nothing to worry about, my business partner paid no attention and didn't come out and see what all the fuss and noise was about.

Dealing with the dynamic between us was one of my very deep-down personal reasons why I'd taken on this adventure. I did not like confrontations and our discussions were always confrontational and I always backed down. I was constantly told that I was wrong, my thoughts were wrong, the way I did things were wrong. I had given this person far too much power over me. It was one of the things I was deciphering on this run. What messages and lessons had I been listening to and living by that were not serving me as an adult? I'd been brought up to respect my elders and to not question or answer back my parents. My business partner was my elder, he was like a father to me and was someone I had respected and looked up to. We had become equal partners in a business, but I deferred to him and had allowed him to push me out.

Part of my WHY for doing this adventure was to prove to myself that I was strong and that I was capable, and in the process of that, I would also prove to myself that I was not the person he thought me to be.

I was given a very good sentence to think about prior to this adventure, it was 'I don't have to prove you wrong to prove me right'.

I went back to this sentence time and time again. I was out to prove me right. I knew that in the process I'd prove others wrong, but first and foremost I was out to prove myself right. I believed it was the stronger, more positive attitude to take.

I was proving myself right and I was feeling good.

Onwards.

Graham walked alongside me as we made our way to the next pub, the Navigation, as we entered, he made quite a loud fuss bellowing out that I was on marathon 61 of 63 in a row. It turned quite a few heads and even better raised quite a bit of cash for the charity.

This was making a pretty awesome day even better.

Sharif, Arwen and Phil were given another 1/3rd of their choice ale, I had a taste and some water. As much as I loved the idea of free beer, I was also very aware that not only did I have to get through the second half of today's marathon, but I also still had another two marathons ahead of me.

There'd be plenty of time to party at the end, for now I still had a job to do.

Sight-seeing and pub-crawling, learning to pull the pints for my team and of course, them drinking their pints was fun, but it was also a bit time-consuming. There were quite a lot of pubs within a short distance of each other and we were taking a bit too long at each.

The day was getting on and at the rate we were going, it was going to be dark before I finished. We had to get a wriggle on and get some distance done between the last city pub and the final two pubs that were back in the suburbs closer to my home.

A bit of a pub diversion was needed so we headed to the Nottingham Horse Racetrack where we were allowed to run along the finish line.

Another flashback memory.

The first time I represented my high school at an inter-school cross-country race was at the Geelong Racecourse, Victoria, Australia. The start of the race was along the strait of the track and then headed out along dirt tracks down to the Barwon River and back.

I remember running my little heart out. Running so hard that I made myself sick. It was a strange feeling of wanting to go as fast as I could, finding my limit and then urging myself to push past it.

I think that was the first time I realised that I could find more inside if I kept going. It was a strange feeling of satisfaction, as well as grossness at the heaving, but definitely satisfaction of giving it everything I had and then some.

We were coming into the final stretch; the last two pubs of the day were what I deemed my locals. The Stratford Haven which is a mile's walk from our house and then the Poppy & Pint, which is a very pleasant kilometre from their door to my home.

The sun had said goodnight by the time we arrived at the Poppy, but I was still a bit short of the full distance. Around and around I ran until finally I cruised towards the pub entrance, arms in the air, the biggest smile on my face, my marathon team – Sharif, Arwen and Phil beside me ...I had officially surpassed the record.

My crazy, ambitious dream had come true.

Graham heralded me in and in his booming voice announced to the crowd, and there was quite a crowd of both pub patrons I didn't know as well as quite a few friendly faces of those that I did, that today I'd completed my 61st marathon in 61 days. Beating the current Guinness World record and that I'd be continuing on to smash it by running two more.

What a cheer!

Friends. Strangers. The staff. My wonderful team. All stood and clapped as I took a bit of a bow and wiped a little tear from my eye.

What a day, which was about to be topped with an open bar and dinner for my team.

Honestly, it was ...

The. Best. Burger. Ever.

I consumed it almost as fast as it arrived, this running sure does work up an appetite.

I had two more marathons to run, but hey my friends didn't, so the beer flowed for them. 61 down, 2 more to go.

DAY 62. RECOVERY MARATHON, NOTTINGHAMSHIRE

Friday 27th October, 2017

Daily distance: 42.4km

Time taken: 6hrs 44mins

Total adventure distance: 2656.3km

I had a few people joining me on this penultimate day. Knowing I was so close and that I'd now completed 2574kms was pretty awesome, but I wasn't complacent.

Our running joke continued 'that I could fall the last little bit' and although in the scheme of the whole adventure they were the last little bits, they still tallied 84.4kms and I didn't really fancy falling 84.4kms – I'd end up with quite a sore butt if that was the case.

I knew what I had to do for the day. Nice and steady and enjoy the company of the team who were going out of their way to make sure I stayed on target and made it to my final day.

The people who joined me each had their own wonderful stories of extraordinary achievements and I was quite happy to listen to and be inspired by them today.

Today was yet another one of my reasons why. I wanted to hear the stories of others, share them with the people who listened to me and show that we all truly have extraordinary within us. Each of us can find a depth to what we can do when we have a passion and a purpose to finding our own personal strengths and keep on going to achieve our own personal goals.

Rob Fenton-Stone had recently completed the Land's End to John O'Groats cycle challenge. Approximately 100 miles per day for 9 days is a spectacular feat. Maintaining that 'I can' attitude when endurance sport is not your usual state of conditioning. This stuff hurts and there is always the option to stop when it gets hard. Finding the willpower to keep going and complete a challenge when your body is screaming at you NOOOOOOO. It is mind-blowing for yourself. It also has an impact beyond you.

People watch. In particular, the younger people watch. Robert is a proud dad to two wonderful kiddos. They watched their dad be a superstar, never giving up, never giving in. This is our legacy to the next generation – when you believe, you can achieve anything you put your mind to.

Clare Biddell is one very understated powerhouse of a woman. I've been very lucky to have run with, and cheered on, Clare during her own crazy adventures. Way back on marathon 38, I attempted to run up Pen Y Fan as the first part of my day. Not only does Clare use this mountain as a hill repeat training venue, but she does also it with a 20kg Bergen on her back.

Clare has completed the Fan Dance more than once, both in the summer and the dreaded winter. The Fan Dance is a trail run which was borne from the training that the SAS endure as part of their program to be the fittest, toughest and the most elite squad in the armed protection service of our country.

Clare's mum died too early in life. Whilst heart-breaking for Clare and her family, it has provided Clare with her zest for a life of purpose, passion and love. She is adamant to make the most of her life, to challenge herself to step out of her comfort zone and give everything she has to see what she's made of and she is made of some pretty tough extraordinary stuff.

Kajsa Tylen is better known for her cycling than running. Kajsa took a year out of her life to sit atop her trusty metallic steed and complete the Guinness World Record for the furthest distance on a bicycle in a year. Not only was there the physicality of cycling her target distance of 90 miles per day for 365 days. The mental challenge of forsaking a normalcy of life – days off, sleep ins, long lunches or dinners with family and friends, all put on hold for an entire year to achieve this crazy dream goal that she had in her head.

People said she couldn't. I had an inkling of what Kajsa had felt when people said that to her. Kajsa ignored the comments and pushed on regardless.

I was so thrilled to be listening to these wonderful stories of personal extraordinary. I listened to the feelings of pride they felt.

Pride is a feeling to harness.

Don't compare yourself to any other. Get inspiration, get ideas that light a fire in your own belly. Then fuel that flame. Take the steps to set up your own personal extraordinary goals and then take the steps to achieve them.

Use your personal drive to find out what you are capable of accomplishing to lift you to your own personal extraordinary level. Feel that pride of knowing that it is your effort that has allowed you to succeed.

Yes, you will have a team of helpers, supporters, cheerers - I could not have done everything that I have done alone. However, it is you who will take all the physical actions to make your dreams come true.

You are worth striving for.

You are worth the effort.

Guess what? We somehow managed to finish marathon 62 at the Poppy & Pint.

It's uncanny really how I could somehow run 42.2kms and somehow manage to finish at a place close to home that provided food and water, with just a touch of alcohol for medicinal purposes. I know I was in no state or mood to cook for myself and I think Sharif was more than happy for someone else to be looking after us.

Post-dinner I was keen to get home, but Sharif asked if I was up for hanging around for one more pint – for him.

I may have grumbled a little – did he not know that I was tired, and I had a rather big day ahead? Apparently, he did, and as he was reminding me that he had actually been aboard the crazy train for the past two months, two people entered the pub.

Strange I thought, that looks quite like Michael and Bridget McNamara. Michael and his wife Sharon are lifelong friends from my hometown Geelong, Australia. Bridget is their eldest daughter.

Wow, these Michael and Bridget doppelgangers were heading towards our table …

Oh, my lordy!

Michael and Bridget McNamara sat at our table.

They had just flown all the way from Melbourne, landed in London, hired a car and driven to Nottingham, booked into a hotel and rushed to the Poppy & Pint over the course of the past 30 hours so that they could join me for my final day.

My mind was blown!

Our tears flowed and a beer was drunk, and whilst I desperately wanted to stay and chat, I knew I had one more thing to do … marathon 63 awaited in the morning.

DAY 63. SWITHLAND WOODS, LEICESTERSHIRE

Saturday 28th October, 2017

Daily distance: 43.1km

Time taken: 9hrs 19mins

Total adventure distance: 2699.4km

Well this had been one doozy of an adventure, hadn't it?

The question 'Could I do something like that?', that had rattled around in my brain since way back in 2009 after reading my two favourite adventure books, was about to be answered.

Seems I could!

Marathon 63 in 63 days was about to become a reality, and as Sharif so eloquently scribbled on our lounge room wall 'You can f**k'n fall this last bit'.

Just as a point, we had covered the entire back wall of our lounge room with whiteboard wallpaper – we called it the Adventure Wall. We used the wall to plan out the 63 days prior to the start so that it was always at the forefront of our minds (and eyes).

Throughout the adventure I scribbled ideas, messages, thoughts, and quotes all over the wall. Sharif wrote me notes most mornings using lines from songs, quotes from books, and many a naughty-worded message to encourage me to get my butt moving.

I was aware that we had a lot of people coming to join me today, but I wasn't exactly sure who. One thing I did know was that my final day had kicked off with a blast from last night's surprise of

Michael and Bridget flying in from Australia to join me, and that today was going to be bit special.

To make it even more memorable for the folk who were going to join me for a little bit of the run, I'd chosen a location where I'd spent sooooo many of my days, weeks, years training around – Swithland Woods.

Apart from knowing these woods like the back of my hand, for those who were going to be using Strava to record their run, they'd receive a lovely little piece of Strava Art to remember the day by.

My route around Swithland Woods is approximately 4-and-a-bit kilometres and produces one of those cute little cartoon sketches of a man's genitalia. Amongst my running friends and training clients its known as my 'nob' run.

To all of those who did join me ... you're welcome.

It was all feeling a little surreal arriving at Swithland Woods, there were people everywhere. Folk from nearby, including Leicester friends, clients and running clubs. Folk from far, gosh people had driven from all over the country to join me. Folk from Australia, this was still blowing my mind. And as I hopped out of the van, one of my besties from childhood, Cindy Boeren, had flown in from the Netherlands to cheer me on.

She'd arrived at East Midlands Airport, caught a taxi to some woods in the actual middle of nowhere carrying a suitcase and arriving before everyone else. The taxi driver asked if she was sure? 'Yep, my mate's running 63 marathons in 63 days and she's finishing here today', was her response. I wonder if the taxi-driver believed her.

Oh man! The tears.

Looking at the crowd and seeing the faces, in particular those of Tamsin Robinson, Mandy Powell and Bridget McNamara who were going to be running their very first marathon distance with me today, I was a bit choked – what a day it was becoming.

I gave a brief little speech, mainly talking about health and safety, for whilst I thought my 'nob' run would be a fitting end to this crazy adventure, the terrain was also pretty tricky. This part I hadn't thought through so much.

When I got home from running through the Peruvian jungle back in June 2016, I thought all systems were go for my 63 marathons adventure. I thought if I could survive Peru then I was pretty invincible. Turns out I wasn't.

I tentatively set a start date for my 63 marathons adventure, drove to the woods to do my first post-jungle / start-63 training run and broke my leg.

This little blip in the road turned out to be one of the best little blips I've had. I had to let my bone heal, which took time. I took the advice of giving myself a minimum of twelve months healing and strengthening time to prepare for the 63 marathons. This all helped me gain a stronger conviction that I would do this, and I also met Sharif in the new timeframe – and let's face it, I'd have never got to marathon 63 without him.

Back to today, we were all ready to run, and so, off we popped to get number 63 done and dusted.

Throughout the day people came and ran with me and my gang of woodland critters. We scootched over tree roots, splashed through creeks, stomped through stinging nettles, Mandy even took on the challenge to crawl under a bridge through a water tunnel – this was a standard exercise I'd get the people I'd trained through the woods to do. Alas, Mandy did go over on her ankle later in the day which slowed her down. It didn't stop her, but the full distance alluded her this day.

For the grand finale, I'd planned that we'd leave the woods and run over and up towards Bradgate Country Park, and then continue running through and up to the top of Old John – as it would be quite a scenic end.

Yes, Nikki, it's scenic because it's at the top of a bloody big hill!

Truly, what was I thinking?

I could see a crowd gathering way up there at the top of Old John, but I'd misjudged the distance just a little. Instead of heading straight up, we had to run the kilometre loop around the bottom of the hill, just a few times.

The sun was dipping, the people were waiting, I was shuffling as fast as I could. Finally, it was time to make the final ascent.

I know I can, I know I can.

My Puffing Billy chant was back, this is the hill I'd shouted it out time and time again to my clients.

The chant ran through my brain on repeat, as the tears formed. I stopped for a quick breather and looked up. There was only a hundred or so metres to the finish line.

I know I can, I know I can.

The chant continued in my head. I had practiced this hill and this chant at least 9,387 times over the past 10 years.

I could hear another chant going on outside my head. 'Let's go Nikki. Let's go' my friends clapped and shouted.

A friendly hand was on my back urging me on. 'Come on Nikki, let's go'.

As I climbed that big hill that I'd put in the way between me and my finish, I glanced at my watches. Finally, they had both ticked over that magical figure 42.2kms.

I'd officially done it!

But I was only halfway up the hill … bugger!

Just a bit little bit more to cross my finish line.

Who's stooopid idea had it been to want to finish up here?

Oh yeah, it was mine!

It was my dream, my ambition, my choice.

I had chosen, of my own free will, to run 63 marathons in 63 days, covering 1677.33 miles or 2699.4 kilometres, and as I crossed my red ribbon finish line to the cheers of my friends, I proved to myself that …

I know I CAN!

THE DAY AFTER THE 63 DAYS BEFORE

So, there we all were, on top of a hill in a country park – only one thing to do, head to the pub.

Sitting in a circle with friends who had travelled from all over the UK and the world was utterly amazing. Colette handed me a little gift – a gold crown and a Hawaiian lei – which I graciously accepted and popped on.

Clocking myself in the mirror standing in my Dryrobe cape, a lei around my neck, a bouquet of flowers in my hand, a crown on my head and tears streaming down my face, I had another little flash-back.

Once upon a time, as well as having wanted to be a ballerina who danced Swan Lake and received rounds of applause and bravos for her performance, I'd also hoped that one day I'd be crowned Miss World (I grew up in the 70's when Miss World was a thing). Standing there, I realised that I had danced with swans, been applauded and bravo'd for my 63in63 performance, and I had just been given a crown for surpassing a World Record.

I looked more Miss Wreck than Miss World, but hey I was one extremely happy Miss Wreck.

We'd been given a complimentary two-night stay at Nottingham Hilton Hotel to celebrate the completion of this adventure. We were greeted on arrival with a note *Miss Love, congratulations on your amazing achievement.* I felt like a superstar ... a knackered superstar who was going to enjoy a great long lay in bed the next day and not run.

Sleep in time – Yay!

Noooooo.

To say I woke in a bit of a panic would be a little understatement.

I should run.

No, I've finished.

But what do I do today? I should run.

No, I've finished.

Go and get some breakfast - but I should run … and so it continued throughout the morning.

Sharif knew I liked to write my thoughts, but I hadn't brought my journal. He popped out and grabbed me a notebook and suggested I write (rather than stress him out).

Since Day 59, I'd been running with this thought in my head *'If it wasn't running skills, what was it that kept me going?'*

With time to reflect, I wrote my answer in my journal.

Thinking back about what I had done to get to the start line and how I'd overcome all the obstacles, I now believe I know the answer …

I used my super-powers!

I am Ambitious, Brave, Committed, Adaptable, Determined, Persistent, Resilient, Proud, Happy, Love

You can call them internal characteristics, but where's the fun in that? I made a commitment to myself to live my life through my filters of Love, Fun and Adventure – so from now on they will be known as my super-powers!

I knew I didn't have to rush out and run another marathon, there were going to be plenty more opportunities.

This was not the end; it was just the start …

THANK YOU

Oh man, I've got soooooo many people to thank for getting me through my 63 marathons in 63 days including everyone who ran with me, put us up overnight, massaged me, provided food and beer and financially supported me on Pledgesport – I hope I mentioned you in the story and from the bottom of my tootsies to the top of my heart I thank you.

Everyone who followed the story on social media and tuned in daily for the 'will she / won't she' episode of Nikki Runs 63 marathons in 63 days – your comments, likes and love carried me through many dark moments. Thank you.

Tamsin Robinson, you offered to give a little of your time to contacting running clubs, schools, media etc., it ended up taking a lot of your time and of course you and your boys took the best care of my little girl Rufus whilst we were on the road. Thank you.

Rona Gibson, after a chance meeting in Glasgow you were on the case championing me within the Hilton Hotel chain. Thank you for organising so many stays for us along the way.

Katie Holmes, you offered to look after my Twitter account and built it up pretty much from a standing start – I still don't get Twitter, but I know it helps spread the word. Thank you.

Dirk and Jane Vervoorts, Arwen Makin, Neil Byford and Jackie Harrison thank you for sharing your stories with me of your life with Huntington's and the ongoing fight to find a cure. Thank you.

Clare Riddell, you and your magic masseuse hands took such good care of my weary body when I was home, your offer to come to my house time and again after you'd finished your work for the day was truly appreciated. Thank you.

Yasin Tayebjee, Osteopath extraordinaire. Healing my body after breaking my leg was not down to chance, it involved all of your

Osteopathic skills to help my bone heal and keep my body in alignment as I trained. Thank you.

To the Rassool family and Unique Window Systems who took up my big investment package on Pledgesport, thank you for your belief and financial support of me, I genuinely appreciated and used every pound that you provided.

Sue and Feroze Owadally, thank you for making and raising a pretty special bloke, for helping us out financially when we were in a bind and feeding us when we were hungry as we chased this crazy dream.

Ruth Pilcher, Tamsin Robinson and Claire McColl, thank you for your eyes and thoughts on the first draft of this book – finding the plot holes, the grammar slips and giving me the feedback that I needed to help me make something I'm proud of.

Becca Papp, my pal who also happens to be a clever psychologist, thank you for helping me build my mental strategies for this adventure … and all the other times I've needed a caring shoulder.

Vivien and Robert Love (mum and dad), you two are my loudest supporters, as well as my biggest worriers. Yes, we often get at loggerheads when I say you shouldn't worry and you say that's your job, but I know that it is always coming from a place of love. Thank you for raising me in love.

To my kiddo Riley, you are my most important extrinsic Why and my most wonderous adventure ever, full stop. I love you.

And last, but absolutely by no means the least, that Bloke, my SuCKER and love, Sharif. I keep saying I don't know how you put up with me, I actually do know the answer to that – it's because of your big heart, your beautiful soul, your kindness and caring, your own ambition and dreams, and because you are you. I am so happy that our life paths crossed and are now running alongside one another – teamwork, togetherness, love, fun and adventure. I love you.

AUTHOR NOTE

I gave thanks on the previous pages to the people that helped me get through my adventure, now it's time to thank you, the awesome reader, for taking the time to purchase this book and hang out with me until the very end of this running adventure tale.

I truly hope you enjoyed our time together as I recanted the experience, and I hope that maybe you are now dreaming, or planning, or about to take off on your own extraordinary adventure. Just before you do though, I'd be very grateful if you could head over to my website and leave a book review.

https://nikkilove.co.uk/product/personalised-signed-copy-of-with-a-little-dash-of-crazy/#reviews

I am an independent author/publisher/adventure runner hoping to spread the word about my book – your reviews help me to do this by showing others that the book has been a worthy read. Thank you.

I've put together a little slideshow of photos from the 63 days and through the magic of photo fairies and this QR code, you can scan this with your phone and you'll be taken on a visual adventure of how I ran 63 marathons in 63 days.

Or you can do it old-school and type in this website address:

https://nikkilove.co.uk/with-a-little-dash-of-crazy-gallery

If you'd like to stay in the loop with where my feet are taking me, what my fingers are writing, or anything ice-cream/cake/beer consumption related, then please do sign up to my Chasing Extraordinary newsletter.

http://nikkilove.co.uk

Note from Sharif: Don't worry, your inbox will not be spammed, Nikki doesn't sit down long enough to write newsletters that often.

Last thing, I share my daily escapades and excessive number of selfies and pooch pics on all the socials, so why not come on over and say howdy on:

Facebook: https://www.facebook.com/nikkijlove

Instagram: https://www.instagram.com/nikkiloveruns/

Twitter: https://twitter.com/nikkiloveruns

x Nikki

CHARITY INFORMATION

**Huntington's
Disease
Association**

The information below has been taken from HDA's website. For further details, please visit www.hda.org.uk

Huntington's Disease is a neuro-degenerative disorder caused by a faulty gene in a person's DNA. It affects a person's nervous system and impacts their movement, learning, thinking and emotions.

It is an inherited disease, and every child conceived naturally to a parent who has the faulty gene has a 50% chance of inheriting it and the disease. It affects men and women and usually develops between the ages of 30 to 50.

Early symptoms may include slight, uncontrollable muscular movements; stumbling and clumsiness; lack of concentration and short-term memory lapses; depression and changes of mood and personality.

The words above have been taken from HDA's website and describe the disease – my friend Dirk, Neil's dad Stuart, Jackie's brother Mark and over 6,000 other people in the UK are the real lives of the disease. Together with their families, they live with it daily knowing that it is progressive and that there is currently no cure.

To anybody with Huntington's or who is impacted with Huntington's, I send you my love and thoughts.

The funding page that I set up for this adventure has now closed, however donations directly to HDA are still welcomed and very much appreciated to help in the fight to find a cure.

https://www.hda.org.uk/donate

Printed in Great Britain
by Amazon